# Translation and Pragmatics

*Translation and Pragmatics* aims to provide a fundamental grounding of key phenomena, theories, and concepts in the field of pragmatics and of some of their manifestations both within and across languages and cultures. The originality of this textbook largely resides in its pedagogical approach which involves familiarising students with the pragmatic phenomena of deixis, speech acts, implicature, and (im)politeness first and foremost through a systematic exposure to concrete, authentic data from a broad spectrum of texts and media (e.g., ads, memes, films, videogames) while showcasing how these phenomena are relayed in different types of translation. With warm-up exercises, illustrative case studies, mini-research activities as well as further reading, this is an essential textbook for translation and intercultural communication students but can also be a useful resource for anyone interested in the interface between pragmatics, translation and/or intercultural communication, media, and the synergies thereof.

**Louisa Desilla** is Assistant Professor in the School of English Language and Literature, Aristotle University of Thessaloniki, Greece. She has co-edited *The Routledge Handbook of Translation and Pragmatics* (2019) and published her research in international academic journals in the fields of linguistics and translation, such as the *Journal of Pragmatics* and *The Translator*.

# Translation and Pragmatics
Theories and Applications

Louisa Desilla

LONDON AND NEW YORK

First published 2025
by Routledge
4 Park Square, Milton Park, Abingdon, Oxon OX14 4RN

and by Routledge
605 Third Avenue, New York, NY 10158

*Routledge is an imprint of the Taylor & Francis Group, an informa business*

© 2025 Louisa Desilla

The right of Louisa Desilla to be identified as author of this work has been asserted in accordance with sections 77 and 78 of the Copyright, Designs and Patents Act 1988.

All rights reserved. No part of this book may be reprinted or reproduced or utilised in any form or by any electronic, mechanical, or other means, now known or hereafter invented, including photocopying and recording, or in any information storage or retrieval system, without permission in writing from the publishers.

*Trademark notice*: Product or corporate names may be trademarks or registered trademarks, and are used only for identification and explanation without intent to infringe.

*British Library Cataloguing-in-Publication Data*
A catalogue record for this book is available from the British Library

ISBN: 978-1-032-08154-0 (hbk)
ISBN: 978-1-032-08150-2 (pbk)
ISBN: 978-1-003-21317-8 (ebk)

DOI: 10.4324/9781003213178

Typeset in Sabon
by Apex CoVantage, LLC

Access the Support Material: www.routledgetranslationstudiesportal.com

To my students: past, present, and future . . .

# Contents

*Preface*     *viii*

**PART I**
**The journey from abstract meaning to contextual meaning and force**     1

1   Deixis: anchoring meaning to real and imaginary worlds     3

2   Speech acts: pinning down communicative intentions     16

**PART II**
**Navigating interpersonal meaning and communicative styles**     29

3   Implicature: reading between the lines     31

4   (Im)politeness: a weapon wielded for better or worse     69

*Index*     *102*

# Preface

In 2019, *The Routledge Handbook of Translation and Pragmatics* was published, edited by Rebecca Tipton and myself. I dedicated that volume to Prof. Elly Ifantidou who, 20 years ago, "introduced me to pragmatics and the fascinating study of how people use language, *inter alia*, to make requests, fight, make amends, negotiate, manipulate and fall in (and out of) love". Had it not been for her own uniquely accessible style of explaining even the most abstract of concepts and showing that pragmatic meaning is actually all around us, in all probability, I would have followed a different research path.

At its heart, this textbook is an attempt to explain as clearly and concretely as possible four salient pragmatic phenomena, primarily catering for the needs and expectations of translation and intercultural communication students who compose its primary target audience. Of course, the textbook may also appeal to researchers who work in the fields of translation and intercultural studies, linguistics, and communication studies. In particular, it can be a useful resource for those interested in the interface between pragmatics, translation, and/or intercultural communication, media, and the synergies thereof.

Perhaps the greatest challenge I faced throughout the writing process is striking a balance between doing justice to the complexity of the pragmatic phenomena examined, and the sophistication of some of the pertinent theories, while at the same time ensuring that the textbook remains accessible and not (too) overwhelming. To this end, it was a conscious decision to give pragmatic theories the leading role with theoretical insights from translation studies playing a supporting role in data analysis. In the second part of the book, readers are more actively encouraged to synthesise information from these two fields and, occasionally, other fields, for that matter. This point brings me to the rationale underlying the book's structure.

The book is divided into two parts. Part I "The Journey from Abstract Meaning to Contextual Meaning and Force" introduces the readers to the pragmatic phenomena of deixis (Chapter 1) and speech acts (Chapter 2). The subtitles of the chapters, i.e., *anchoring meaning to real and imaginary worlds* and *pinning down communicative intentions*, respectively, reflect the first two milestones in the process of understanding pragmatic meaning:

contextual meaning and speaker meaning. Part II "Navigating Interpersonal Meaning and Communicative Styles" deals with the more complex albeit very intriguing phenomena of implicature and (im)politeness, bringing into sharp relief their pivotal role in shaping the style of the communication as well as the relationship between interactants. In fact, the titles and subtitles of most chapters can be thought of as pointers to key aspects of pragmatic competence and, in a way, represent the skills that translators need to actively develop further.

All chapters have the same structure for the sake of reader-friendliness: they start with a thought-provoking **warm-up exercise**, followed by the explanation of **key concepts** and theories drawing mostly on attested examples, e.g., from films, social networking sites, advertisements, memes, etc. Importantly, in each chapter there is one case study investigating the pragmatic phenomenon in question in the context of translation and demonstrating how relevant theories and/or models can be applied in practice. A gloss or back-translation is always used for data in languages other than English. Through these **illustrative case-studies**, which are designed to increase in complexity and length as the book progresses, as well as through the **mini exercises and research activities** and the **suggestions for further reading** at the end of each chapter, readers are given the opportunity to experience how pragmatic phenomena are realised and negotiated in established and new types of translation such as film subtitling, audio-description, transcreation, and videogame localisation.

By way of concluding this preface, I would like to thank the anonymous reviewer who helped improve parts of the manuscript. I would also like to express my gratitude to Dr Evangelia Liakou, researcher in media accessibility and audio-describer, who has granted me permission to use a short excerpt from the audio-description she created for the purposes of her PhD research (Liakou, 2021).

Part I

# The journey from abstract meaning to contextual meaning and force

# 1 Deixis
## Anchoring meaning to real and imaginary worlds

## 1.1 Warm-up

Consider the following utterances:

- "Depart here for Winter Wonderland, or as I like to call it, how to spend a lot of money very quickly".
- "If you're popping upstairs, please have a word with the Big Man because we need all the help we can get today".

Can you make any guesses about the speaker and the addressee(s) of these? Who could they be? Where and when could these utterances be produced?

Is there anything that you would need to know or look up if you were to translate them in one of your working languages?

## 1.2 Key concepts

### 1.2.1 From abstract meaning to utterance meaning

Understanding utterance meaning is a process that most of us engage in several times a day, e.g., while interacting face to face, chatting on social media, reading a book, watching our favourite series, playing videogames, or following a recipe when cooking dinner. As Cummings (2023: 1) aptly remarks, "[L]anguage is a vehicle through which we express our thoughts and desires, negotiate relationships with others, and reflect on situations that cause us joy, sadness and a wide range of emotions". Yet, overall we seem to be almost blissfully unaware of the intricacies of pragmatic competence and tend to take for granted that our brain will be able to successfully carry out an array of pertinent cognitive tasks at lightning speed every single time. Translators may well be more in tune with these mechanisms as they embark on the quest of deciphering meaning on a completely different – and more conscious – level, but usually most people would take a step back and analyse how they have understood an utterance only when a communicative breakdown happens. Having said that, taking into account the complex nature of utterance

DOI: 10.4324/9781003213178-2

# 4 *From abstract meaning to contextual meaning and force*

interpretation, it is surprising that misunderstandings are the exception rather than the rule (Cummings, 2023). Aside from pragmatic language disorders, in which virtually every interaction is very likely to end up in misunderstandings and unfulfilled communicative goals, the majority of interactants overall navigate fairly smoothly the inferential tasks involved in utterance comprehension (ibid). Understanding propositional meaning is the first milestone in this journey. Context plays a crucial role because it considerably delimits the meaning potential of an utterance and, indeed, interactants intuitively look for contextual cues (Thomas, 1995) in their attempt to make sense of what is said. What happens when there is no or limited access to context, though?

Let us revisit the utterances in the warm-up exercise. With no access whatsoever to the context in which they were produced, it is impossible to know specifically and precisely what (a) and (b) mean. Put differently, we are unable to recover the *proposition expressed*, which corresponds to the basic statement asserted by the speaker. Proposition refers to that part of the meaning which leads to a complete and clear account of a state of affairs in the external reality (Hurford & Heasly, 1983: 89). It is essential that this account can be assigned a truth-value (ibid). In order to determine whether what the speaker said is true or false, addressee(s) need to compare it to the state of affairs in the external world. To this end, two key pragmatic processes need to be performed: *disambiguation*, and *reference assignment* (Thomas, 1995; Scott, 2022). For instance, out of context the linguistic expression "Winter Wonderland", represented in writing with upper case initials, could be linked to the external world in several ways: it could be any of the Christmas events held in cities around the world, featuring festive markets as well as numerous attractions and activities including theme park rides, ice-skating, etc.; or it could be the title of the classic Christmas song; or the title of an American 1946 film, to mention only a few possibilities. In the case of the utterance in (a), co-text itself restricts the range of these possibilities; due to the presence of "here" and the "how to spend money very quickly" remark, we can safely assume that Winter Wonderland is a place rather than a film or a song. But then another question arises: to which Winter Wonderland is the speaker referring? Unless we have access to information regarding the precise geographical location in which the utterance is produced, we cannot answer this question. The adverb "here" is not particularly helpful either. Perhaps we can assume that this place must be somewhere where English is spoken, but again, this leaves us with large number of 'candidate' cities in several countries. A similar conundrum occurs in the case of "Big Man" in (b) which means different things in different contexts. For some, the lexical item "upstairs" preceding "Big Man", in tandem with the comment that "we need all the help we can get", might bring to mind the expression "The Big Man upstairs" which refers to God in Heaven or a deity living in a place up above (www.urbandictionary.com/define.php?term=the%20big%20man%20 upstairs). If we entertain this assumption, what would "popping upstairs" mean then? Dying and going to Heaven?

*Deixis* 5

It is high time that the contexts of these utterances were revealed; both (a) and (b) are allegedly uttered by London underground drivers addressing passengers (Noble, 2016). Based on this information, it becomes clear that the driver in (a) actually refers to Hyde Park Winter Wonderland. Nevertheless, it is difficult to work out exactly which Tube station is denoted by "here" since Hyde Park Winter Wonderland can be accessed via more than one station: although the nearest step-free station is Green Park, Winter Wonderland can be accessed via Hyde Park Corner, Knightsbridge, Victoria Bond Street, Paddington, and Marble Arch, depending on the attraction that one wishes to visit. When it comes to the Tube station referred to by the driver in (b) there is an even wider range of options. Had it not been for the addition of the contextual information "At Saint Paul's" (Noble, 2016) by the person posting the utterance in question, we would have still been nonplussed.

Whether appreciating the sardonic humour in (a) and the playfulness in (b) or not, in all probability, the comprehension process of the two utterances would have been less arduous for the Tube passengers themselves because they were physically there: they were on board the train at that particular moment in time listening to the driver's station announcements. By virtue of being physically present, they had a much better chance at identifying the referent of the linguistic expressions "here", "upstairs", "you", and "we". Lexical items like these 'pick out' or 'point to' elements in the context of an utterance and generally pass unnoticed unless we feel that they hinder communication (Cummings, 2023). This indexical function is referred to as *deixis* originating from the Ancient Greek word δείξις which means *pointing* (Marmaridou, 2000; Yule, 2020). Encoded by specific linguistic expressions, deixis seems to lie on the borderline between semantics and pragmatics (Carston, 1998) but due to its intimate link with context can be more thoroughly catered for within pragmatics; it is treated as a pragmatic phenomenon because it "motivates the construction of communicatively and socio-culturally defined roles human beings take" in a communicative event (Marmaridou, 2000: 116).

### 1.2.2 Categories of deixis and reference

In Lyons's (1977: 637) definition, *deixis* encompasses

> the location and identification of person, objects, events, processes and activities being talked about or referred to, in relation to the spatiotemporal context created and sustained by the act of utterance and the participation in it, typically, of a single speaker and at least one addressee.

In this light, deictic expressions fall under three basic categories: *person deixis*, *place deixis*, and *time deixis*. This traditional account has been complemented by additional categories, including *social deixis* and *discourse deixis* as well as three secondary types such as *empathetic deixis* (e.g., the use of *this* and *that* to indicate emotional or other psychological proximity

## 6 From abstract meaning to contextual meaning and force

distance respectively between a speaker and a referent), *perceptual deixis* (as in "There's Harry"), and *delivery deixis* (as in "Here's your pizza") (Marmaridou, 2000: 69; cf. Lyons, 1977; Lakoff, 1987). In what follows, the focus will be on illustrating the five basic types of deixis, bearing in mind that the aforementioned categorisation is rather rigid and, therefore, does not do complete justice to the complexity of the phenomenon when analysing empirical data (ibid).

To begin with, deictic relationships are organised around the *origo* which is a construct used by Bühler (1934) to describe the *here*, the *now*, and the *me* of the communication. *Origo* means 'origin' in Latin, so for Bühler it essentially encapsulates the origins of a communicative event. The referent of the pronoun 'I' is the speaker as s/he is placed at the centre of the origo. Unless otherwise specified, the terms *speaker* and *communicator* are used interchangeably throughout this textbook. Hence, a speaker can be a Tube driver making an announcement, a film character, or the creator of an online meme. Accordingly, the term *addressee(s)* or *audience* describes the other key participant in a communicative event which is the referent of 'you'. Now, the addressee may be a clearly identifiable person (e.g., a neighbour that we say good morning to at the local grocery), the Tube passengers listening to the driver's announcement, a film audience, or an online audience which may include billions of potential viewers of a particular meme.

Deictic words such as *I* and *you* are prototypical examples of person deixis. *Person* and *social deixis* are best treated together, since the former can overlap with social relationships between interactants (Cummings, 2023). In a number of languages, social relationships are encoded in the pronoun system; for instance, the choice between *tu/vous* in French, *du/Sie* in German, εσύ/εσείς in Greek, *tu/Lei* in Italian, *ty/vy* in Russian, and *tú/usted* in Spanish will reflect the social distance between speaker and addressee (Baker, 2011). Japanese is yet another language in which the person system is equipped to account for different possibilities regarding levels of intimacy and social status (Levinson, 1983). Unlike these languages, English does not have a formality/deference dimension in its person system; the same deictic *you* would be used to cater for all the potential social relationships between interactants. In English, the latter are signalled mainly through other lexical choices, such as first names (e.g., 'Louisa') as opposed to last names preceded by an honorific (e.g., 'Dr Desilla' or 'Ms. Desilla'). When used as vocatives, these linguistic expressions co-exist with the pronoun *you* in an utterance (e.g., Dr Desilla, are you a medical doctor?) and clearly serve a deictic function (Cummings, 2023). The aforementioned difference between English and other languages has important implications for translation and interpreting; for example, when translating person deixis from English into French, German, Greek, Japanese, Italian, and Russian, decisions will need to be made along the social distance dimension and context may or may not be helpful in this respect (Baker, 2011). In a similar vein, Díaz-Cintas and Remael (2021) stress that "subtitlers will have to resort to other visual, linguistic and narrative clues in the source film to determine the relationship between characters; they might have to ask themselves questions like 'for how long have these two people known each other'?" A micro-level choice such as the one between 'tu' and 'vous' can have salient narrative ramifications because it is directly linked to characterisation (Guillot, 2014).

Apart from *person deixis*, *time* and *place* deixis play a pivotal role in anchoring a communicative event to a real or fictional world. As far as place deixis is concerned, adverbs such as *here* and demonstrative noun phrases like *this hotel* are used to indicate locations that are proximal to the speaker, while distal locations are encoded by adverbs such as *there* and *upstairs*, and phrases like *that restaurant*. Place deixis is used effectively when the communicator is not only well aware of his/her location but also has at least a rough idea of the addressee(s)' location at a given moment in time (Cummings, 2023). As Marmaridou (2000: 87) observes, in so far as the communicator's location may be different at different times, "place deixis automatically incorporates a temporal aspect of the speech event". Adverbs like *now, then, today*, and *tomorrow* as well as adverbial phrases such as *next week, last year, in a minute*, and *late November* exemplify time deixis. Because there are variations in the conceptualisation and the linguistic representation of space and time across cultures (Filipović & Jaszczolt, 2012; Jackson, 2014), place and time deixis require careful handling in translation and intercultural communication, in general. What is more, because the time of publication/ reception or an original text is more often than not earlier than that of its translation, deictic expressions encoding time and or/place might need to be adjusted accordingly.

So far we have illustrated 'deixis proper'; in other words, the focus was on deictic expressions that look outside the utterance for reference, namely to an extralinguistic real or imaginary world. Some of these same expressions (e.g., pronouns, adverbs) can also look inside the utterance or in the wider co-text surrounding the utterance (Cummings, 2023). This phenomenon is called *anaphora* i.e., referring back (Yule, 2020). In the utterance, "Depart here for Winter Wonderland, or as I like to call it, how to spend a lot of money very quickly", the pronoun "it" refers back to "Winter Wonderland". The first mention "Winter Wonderland" is the *antecedent* whereas "it" is the anaphoric expression. A much less common pattern of reference is called *cataphora*, i.e., referring forward, when the anaphoric expression precedes the antecedent (Yule, 2020: 154). Cataphoric reference could look like this: "It is London's most popular Christmas destination. Winter Wonderland is back!" Cataphora is commonly used as an attention-getting device and/or for the sake of maintaining suspense (Yule, 2020: 154). From a cohesion perspective, Baker (2011) offers an insightful discussion of patterns of reference in different languages, demonstrating *inter alia*, that (a) some languages show a preference to pronouns as vehicles of anaphora while others prefer to repeat the initial referring expression (e.g., a proper name) and (b) translators need to become familiar with the variation of reference patterns across genres, as well.

# 8 *From abstract meaning to contextual meaning and force*

As Scott (2022) points out, forward reference is used to great effect in clickbait headlines because it helps create an information gap, thus arousing curiosity.

---

**Headline Examples:**

a) EN: The flavor of Haribo's green gummy bear will shock you! (Keller, 2023)

b) EL: Επιτέλους το παραδέχτηκαν: Αποκαλύφθηκε η πραγματική γεύση που έχει το πράσινο ζελεδάκι της Haribo. (Πασπαλιάρη, 2023)
[At last they admitted it: the true flavour of the green Haribo jelly was revealed.]

c) FR: Voici le VÉRITABLE goût des nounours verts Haribo . . . et ce n'est pas la pomme! (*Marie France*, 2023)
[Here is the REAL flavour of Haribo green teddy bears . . . and it's not apple!]

d) SE: Det här visste du inte om Haribos gummibjörn – avslöjandet chockar alla. (Norberg, 2023)
[Here's what you didn't know about Haribo's gummy bears – the revelation shocks everyone.]

---

Examples (a) to (d) are headlines of articles published between 17 April and 22 April 2023 reporting on the revelation that the green-coloured gummy bear of an internationally well-known confectionary brand is actually strawberry and not apple or lime as many would have thought. Although newspaper headlines are attention-grabbing devices, they also need to be approached as autonomous, self-contained texts (Dor, 2003; Ifantidou, 2009). Regardless of whether all four headlines given were originally intended as clickbait or not, we will treat them as such because they seem to exhibit the distinctive strategies of clickbait headlines which "exploit our pragmatic processing systems to create a promise of information that many find irresistible" (Scott, 2022: 128). These strategies include sensationalist language (e.g., "shock", "the REAL flavour") and suspenseful language (e.g., "and it's not apple") deftly woven with different categories of deixis for the sake of arousing curiosity: the readers are addressed directly in the English and the Swedish headlines in which the personal pronouns "you" and "du" are used respectively. It is noteworthy that "du" encodes a single person addressee (as opposed to "ni" which is the plural "you"), while the English "you" could be either. In any case, through this use of person deixis, readers are encouraged to feel that they actually belong to the intended audience and, by extension, that they will learn something of interest (Scott, 2022). The French and the Swedish headlines illustrate yet another device contributing to the information

Deixis 9

gap, namely the use of the forward-referring "voici" and "här". Earlier in this chapter, the adverb *here* was described as a place deictic expression; however, because in this case *here's* points to the main part of the article (and not to the external world), it serves as a *discourse-deictic* expression.

As Scott explains, *here's* can be teasingly used to arouse the reader's curiosity by implying that that information exists without actually providing the information itself" (2022: 140); in order to gain full access to this promised, enlightening piece of news, he/she has to keep reading.

## 1.3 Case study

As shown in section 1.2., interpreting utterances with no access to their socio-physical context can be an impossible task. Accordingly, translating without context is a futile endeavour (Baker, 2011). It is as if we grope towards meaning in the dark. What happens, though, when addressees have very limited or no access to context due to a visual impairment? The following case study encapsulates the importance of deixis in audio-description (AD) for the blind and partially sighted, drawing on real AD data from Liakou (2021) as well as an interview with researcher and audio-describer Dr Evangelia Liakou, specifically conducted for the purposes of this chapter.

Audio description, henceforth referred to as AD, for the blind/partially sighted and subtitling for the D/deaf and hard-of-hearing (SDH) are the two principal modes of media accessibility, belonging to the broader field of audiovisual translation (AVT). AD is

> an enabling service for blind and partially sighted audiences . . . describing clearly, vividly and succinctly what is happening on screen . . . in the silent intervals between . . . dialogue in order to convey the principal visual elements of a production.
> (RNIB definition cited in Holland, 2009: 170)

AD helps people with partial or complete sight loss access audiovisual media and is also available in museums, opera houses, and theatres, as well as in sports events (Fryer, 2016: 1). It should be noted that the target audience of AD is considerably varied, since it potentially also includes sighted viewers who find it useful, such as language learners and neurodiverse people. Reviers and Vercauteren (2013, n.p.) highlight that AD needs to make audiovisual products such as films not only accessible but also enjoyable "by transferring images into a verbal narration that interacts with the dialogues and sounds of the original text with which it forms a coherent whole". Hence, AD is at its very core a form of *intersemiotic translation* (Jacobson, 1959/2004). Turning images into words is by no means a straightforward process because we are dealing with two different semiotic systems that make meaning in their own ways. Since its birth, cinema has been celebrated first and foremost as a visual medium owing to the great expressive powers of the moving image (Kozloff,

## 10  From abstract meaning to contextual meaning and force

2000: 4). Apart from making the film visually attractive, the *mise-en-scène* (which includes setting props, costumes, lighting, and acting) serves salient narrative functions: it anchors the film to space and time and reveals character (e.g., age, gender, profession, cultural background, emotional state, etc.) (Borwell & Thomson, 1997; Dix, 2008). Audio-describers need to ensure that salient elements of the *mise-en-scène* are conveyed in the AD so that blind and partially sighted audiences can establish where and when the film is set (including any travels across time and space) and become familiar with the characters.

According to Fryer (2016: 58), AD has two modes: "a narration mode" addressing the critical questions of *who*, *what*, *where*, and *when* and "a description mode" which focuses on the *how*, filling in the visual detail. These two modes cater for the 'need to know' and the 'nice to know' elements, respectively (ibid). Since AD must not overlap with the original dialogue or voice-over, information about the film's setting and characters as well as cinematographic style and cast and crew is sometimes offered in an audio-introduction (AI), which is a short piece or narration (with an average duration of 5–7 min. for the cinema) which precedes the start of a film (Fryer, 2019). Importantly, AIs "replicate the effect of vision" since they provide contextual information (ibid: 433). This presupposes a skilful use of person, space, and time deixis as well as anaphora. The following excerpts of the AI specifically designed by Liakou (2021) as part of her reception study of the Greek film *Το Τανγκό των Χριστουγέννων* (*The Tango of Christmas*, 2011) are good cases in point (a gloss in English is provided after the Greek original):

*Η ταινία διαδραματίζεται <u>αρχικά</u> στη <u>σύγχρονη χριστουγεννιάτικη Αθήνα</u> και μια μεγάλη αναδρομή <u>μάς</u> μεταφέρει <u>σε ένα στρατόπεδο του Έβρου, Χριστούγεννα του 1970</u>. Τα γυρίσματα της ταινίας πραγματοποιήθηκαν στην <u>Αλίαρτο Βοιωτίας, το Διδυμότειχο, την Καρωτή Έβρου</u> και <u>την Αθήνα</u>. Πρόκειται για μια ατμοσφαιρική ταινία με καλλιγραφική και έντονα καλλιτεχνική διάθεση, που δίνει ιδιαίτερη βαρύτητα στο σκηνικό που περιβάλλει την πλοκή, στη βροχή, στην ομίχλη, στο καραφλό τοπίο που αγκαλιάζει <u>το στρατόπεδο</u>.*

    . . .

*<u>Στη χριστουγεννιάτικη Αθήνα του σήμερα</u>, ένας ηλικιωμένος πρώην φαντάρος, ο Λάζαρος Λαζάρου, θα έρθει αντιμέτωπος με το παρελθόν του. <u>Εμείς</u> τον ακολουθούμε στην αναδρομή του <u>πίσω στο 1970, σε ένα στρατόπεδο του Έβρου</u> όπου υπηρετούσε νέος, 25 ετών περίπου, ένα συνεσταλμένο, ταπεινό, μαζεμένο παιδί με μεγάλα, ευγενικά, καστανά μάτια. <u>Εκεί</u> θα γνωρίσουμε τον υπολοχαγό <u>του</u>, Στέφανο Καραμανίδη, έναν στιβαρό άντρα γύρω στα 35, ψηλό, με μουστάκι, σκούρα καστανά μαλλιά και διαπεραστικό βλέμμα. <u>Στο ίδιο στρατόπεδο</u> θα συναντήσουμε τον συνταγματάρχη Μανώλη Λόγγο, διοικητή του στρατοπέδου, έναν σκληρό στρατιωτικό, που βάζει το καθήκον πάνω απ' όλα.*

*Deixis* 11

[*In the beginning*, the movie takes place in <u>*contemporary Athens at*</u> <u>*Christmas time*</u> and a long flashback transfers <u>*us*</u> <u>*to an army camp in*</u> <u>*Evros, at Christmas in 1970*</u>. The filming took place <u>*in Aliartos (Vio-*</u> <u>*tia), Didymoteicho, Karoti (Evros) and Athens*</u>. This is an atmospheric film, with an exceptionally artistic and calligraphic style and with em- phasis on the setting where the plot unravels, the rain, the mist, the fog, the bald landscape enveloping <u>*the camp*</u>.

. . .

<u>*In present-day Athens, at Christmastime*</u>, an elderly ex-soldier, Laza- ros Lazarou, will come face-to-face with his past. <u>*We*</u> follow him, as <u>*he*</u> flashbacks to 1970, <u>*to an army camp in Evros*</u>, where <u>*he*</u> served at 25; a reserved, humble, quiet boy with big, gentle, brown eyes. <u>*There, we*</u> will meet <u>*his*</u> lieutenant, Stephanos Karamanidis, a robust, tall man, around 35, with mustache, brown hair and piercing eyes. <u>*In the same camp*</u> <u>*we*</u> will also meet Colonel Manolis Loggos, commander of the camp. <u>*He*</u> is a tough military man who puts duty above all else].

From the perspective of person deixis, the prevalent use of the pronoun 'we' in the AI excerpts above is particularly noteworthy. The audience, i.e., blind and partially sighted viewers, are not addressed directly by means of 'you'. 'We' gives the impression that audio-describer and audience embark upon the journey of film viewing together, thus creating intimacy and solidarity. Furthermore, the audio-describer thought that it was essential to explicitly communicate to the audience the flashback that takes place in the film: from "contemporary Athens at Christmas time" we travel back "to an army camp in Evros, at Christmas in 1970". In fact, towards the end of the film, we return to the present day (or, more accurately, what is portrayed as present day in the film), so the audience, through the AI, is given the opportunity to be sensitised to this travelling across time and space. The references to spe- cific shooting locations might seem of secondary importance at first glance, but, in tandem with the evocative description at the end of the first excerpt, can help with the visualisation of the atmospheric setting of Evros on the north-eastern border of Greece. Another feature of the present AI that should not be ignored pertains to the careful handling of anaphora when introduc- ing characters: in line with standard AD practices (Fryer, 2016), pronouns are used as anaphoric expressions only when the identity of the referent can be readily identified in the immediately previous sentence in order to mini- mise the risk of confusion. Cohesion, which operates on more than one level here owing to the intersemiotic nature of the AD (Di Giovanni, 2014), is also established through lexical repetition (i.e., "to an army camp", "in the camp", "of the camp"). The audience is thus strongly encouraged to estab- lish a clear and solid sense of place at least for the main action of the film.

Although studies on AD within the field of audiovisual translation (AVT) have gained momentum over the last decade (Perego, 2019), research on the pragmatics of AD is extremely scarce (Fryer, 2019). On the basis of the

## 12 *From abstract meaning to contextual meaning and force*

above, it seems that deixis is a pragmatic phenomenon worth investigating in the context of AD. For instance, it would be interesting to shed some light on the way professional audio-describers view the role of deixis in AD as well as on any challenges they may face in this respect. To this end, I conducted the following interview with Dr Evangelia Liakou, researcher in AD and professional audio-describer, in which she also comments on the reception of the AI for the Greek film *Το Τανγκό των Χριστουγέννων* (*The Tango of Christmas*) by blind audiences as part of her PhD research (Liakou, 2021):

1) **Based on your experience as a researcher in AD and audio-describer, how important do you think the role of deixis (person, spatial, temporal) is in AD and why?**

   The international guidelines in AD clearly state that the explicit statement of *Who, What, Where, When* is paramount in each audio described scene. In my research, I tested this theory and verified the need to have this information clearly stated in the beginning of each scene. Even in scenes where these elements would be identified my other diegetic features (soundtrack, dialogue etc.), the audience preferred to have the information given through the AD, rather than try and figure it out themselves, compromising their enjoyment and risking breaking the engagement with the audiovisual product.

2) **What was the target audience's overall response to the treatment of spatial and temporal deixis in the audio introduction (AI) that you have designed as part of your reception study (Λιάκου, 2021) of the film *Το Ταγκό των Χριστουγέννων* (Κουτελιδάκης, 2011)?**

   The majority of the audience found the AI helpful and necessary, although they stated that they would have probably understood and enjoyed the content without it as well. The information on time and space given in the AI helped prepare the audience for the flashback in the film (the flashback was explicitly mentioned in the AI). Overall, based on their responses, there was a sense that the references to the setting/location were less important than the temporal references; most appreciated the fact that they were prepared for the flashback.

3) **Describe a time when catering for deixis (person/spatial/temporal) in the main AD script of a film proved rather challenging. What was the nature of the challenge (e.g., lexical choice, cinematography/editing, spatiotemporal constraints) and how did you tackle it?**

   There were many instances during the composition of the AD script and the timecoding of said script that problems regarding catering for deixis emerged. The most common reason was the spatiotemporal limitations. Preferably *who, when, where* are stated in the beginning of each scene, so the audience can keep track and have a context in which the plot will unravel. On many occasions, there was a scene or shot change and there was not enough space to state everything (usually because the dialogue started right away, more seldom because the music and sound effects were

*Deixis* 13

too important to be muffled by the AD). The way to tackle this issue was to prioritize and add the remaining info in the second available gap, e.g. we state the time (*the next morning*), and we add the *who* and *where* right after the 'obstacle' (most commonly dialogue).

For example, (hypothetical scenario):

[scene change]
[AD] *The next morning*
Maria: So, how come you came by?
[AD] *Maria is at home, talking on the phone*

Another way to tackle spatiotemporal constraints is to use shorter deictic expressions (e.g., instead of *the next morning* we just state *morning)* or use shorter synonyms/properties (instead of *Commander's house* we can say *Colonel's house* or instead of *police headquarters* we can say *police station*). Lastly, if none of the above solutions are available, (for instance because the next available gap for AD after the beginning of the scene is too late in the scene or no condensation or substitution is possible), then we need to prioritise; taking into account which features can be understood by the other channels so we can omit them, e.g., the person is easily identifiable by the dialogue.

## 1.4   Exercises and mini research activities

1) Compile a small corpus of clickbait headlines in English and another one in one of your other working languages. What categories of deixis and patterns of reference can you observe? Compare and contrast the two corpora in terms of the above.
2) Watch Trailer A[1] and Trailer B[2]:

  • How does the use of deixis in the AD of the ballet trailer compare to that of the videogame trailer?
  • Do deixis and reference in the AD support or hinder cohesion in the two trailers? Justify your answer drawing on examples of both intra-textual cohesion (i.e., within the AD itself) and intersemiotic cohesion (i.e., between the AD, the visuals, and/or the original soundtrack).

## 1.5   Suggestions for further reading

*On the concept of deixis:*

Cummings, L. (2023) *Introducing Pragmatics: A Clinical Approach*, Oxon and New York: Routledge, Chapter 4.
Lyons, J. (1977) *Semantics: Vols I and II*, Cambridge: Cambridge University Press, Chapter.
Marmaridou, S. (2000) *Pragmatic Meaning and Cognition*, Amsterdam and Atlanta: John Benjamins, Chapter.

## 14 From abstract meaning to contextual meaning and force

*On deixis/reference in translation:*

Baker, M. (2011) *In Other Words: A Coursebook on Translation*, Oxon and New York: Routledge, Sections 4.2.3, Chapter 6.

Liao, M.H. (2011) 'Interaction in the Genre of Popular Science', *The Translator* 17(2): 349–368.

Mason, I., & Şerban, A. (2003) 'Deixis as an Interactive Feature in Literary Translations from Romanian into English', *Target International Journal of Translation Studies* 15(2): 269–294.

## Notes

1 https://www.youtube.com/watch?v=Ukcu2oL2-is
2 https://www.youtube.com/watch?v=S0HfmLjMksY

## References

Baker, M. (2011) *In Other Words: A Coursebook on Translation*, Oxon and New York: Routledge.

Bordwell, D., & Thomson, K. (1997) *Film Art.* 5th edition, New York: McGraw-Hill.

Bühler, K. (1934) *Sprachtheorie*, Jena: Fischer.

Carston, R. (1998) 'The Semantics/Pragmatics Distinction: A View from Relevance Theory', *UCL Working Papers in Linguistics* 10.

Cummings, L. (2023) *Introducing Pragmatics: A Clinical Approach*, Oxon and New York: Routledge.

Díaz-Cintas, J., & Remael, A. (2021) *Subtitling: Concepts and Practices*, Oxon and New York: Routledge.

Di Giovanni, E. (2014) 'Audio Description and Textuality', *PARALLÈLES* 26: 69–83. Geneva: University of Geneva.

Dix, A. (2008) *Beginning Film Studies*, Manchester and New York: Manchester University Press.

Dor, D. (2003) 'On Newspaper Headlines as Relevance Optimizers', *Journal of Pragmatics* 35: 695–721. https://doi.org/10.1016/S0378-2166(02)00134-0

Filipović, L., & Jaszczolt, K.M. (2012) 'Introduction: Linguistic Diversity in the Spatio-Temporal Domain', in L. Filipović & K.M. Jaszczolt (eds.), *Space and Time in Languages and Cultures: Language, Culture, and Cognition*, Amsterdam and Philadelphia: John Benjamins.

Fryer, L. (2016) *An Introduction to Audio Description: A Practical Guide*, Oxon and New York: Routledge.

Fryer, L. (2019) 'Stating the Obvious? Implicature, Explicature and Audiodescription', in R. Tipton & L. Desilla (eds.), *The Routledge Handbook of Translation and Pragmatics*, Oxon and New York: Routledge, 430–445.

Guillot, M. (2014) 'Film Subtitles from a Cross-cultural Pragmatics Perspective: Issues of Linguistic and Cultural Representation', *The Translator* 16(1): 67–92.

Holland, A. (2009) 'Audio Description in the Theatre and the Visual Arts: Images into Words', in J. Díaz-Cintas & G. Anderman (eds.), *Audiovisual Translation*, London: Palgrave Macmillan, 170–185. https://doi.org/10.1057/9780230234581_13

Hurford, J.R., & Heasly, B. (1983) *Semantics: A Coursebook*, Cambridge: Cambridge University Press.

Ifantidou, E. (2009) 'Newspaper Headlines and Relevance: Ad Hoc Concepts in Ad Hoc Contexts', *Journal of Pragmatics* 41(4): 699–720. https://doi.org/10.1016/j.pragma.2008.10.016

*Deixis* 15

Jackson, J. (2014) *Introducing Language and Intercultural Communication*, Oxon and New York: Routledge.

Jacobson, R. (1959/2004) 'On Linguistic Aspects of Translation', in L. Venuti (ed.), *The Translation Studies Reader*. 2nd edition, Amsterdam and Philadelphia: John Benjamins, 138–143.

Keller, E. (2023) '"Haribo Fans Shocked to Learn Green Gummy Bear Flavor": Calling the Police', *The New York Post*. Available at: https://nypost.com/2023/04/17/haribo-fans-shocked-to-learn-green-gummy-bear-flavor-calling-the-police/ (Accessed date: 5 December 2023).

Kozloff, S. (2000) *Overhearing Film Dialogue*, Berkeley, CA: University of California Press

Lakoff, G. (1987) *Women, Fire and Dangerous Things: What Categories Reveal about the Mind*, Chicago and London: The University of Chicago Press.

Levinson, S.C. (1983) *Pragmatics*, Cambridge: Cambridge University Press.

Liakou, E. (2021) *Audio Description Techniques for Greek Cinema*. PhD thesis submitted to the Department of Foreign Languages, Translation and Interpreting, Ionian University of Corfu. Available at: www.didaktorika.gr/eadd/handle/10442/49679?locale=en (Accessed date: 4 December 2023).

Lyons, J. (1977) *Semantics: Vols I and II*, Cambridge: Cambridge University Press.

Marie France (2023) *Voici le VÉRITABLE goût des nounours verts Haribo . . . et ce n'est pas la pomme!*. Available at: www.mariefrance.fr/actualite/veritable-gout-nounours-verts-haribo-pomme-764613.html#item=3 (Accessed date: 5 December 2023).

Marmaridou, S. (2000) *Pragmatic Meaning and Cognition*, Amsterdam and Atlanta: John Benjamins.

Noble, W. (2016) *The Funniest Things You've Heard Tube Drivers Say*. Available at: https://londonist.com/2015/01/the-funniest-things-youve-heard-tube-drivers-say (Accessed date: 5 December 2023).

Norberg, L. (2023) 'Det här visste du inte om Haribos gummibjörn – avslöjandet chockar alla', *Häntnyheter*. Available at: www.hant.se/nyheter/smaken-pa-haribos-grona-gummibjorn-chockar-alla/9513435 (Accessed date: 5 December 2023).

Perego, E. (2019) 'Audio Description: Evolving Recommendations for Usable, Effective and Enjoyable Practices', in L. Pérez González (ed.), *The Routledge Handbook of Audiovisual Translation Studies*, Oxon and New York: Routledge, 114–129.

Reviers, N., & Vercauteren, G. (2013) *The Basics of Audio Description: An Introductory Workshop*, Berlin. https://doi.org/10.7202/1037746ar

Scott, K. (2022) *Pragmatics Online*, Oxon and New York: Routledge.

Thomas, J. (1995) *Meaning in Interaction. An Introduction to Pragmatics*, London: Longman.

Yule, G. (2020) *The Study of Language*. 7th edition, New York: Cambridge University Press.

Πασπαλιάρη, Ε. (2023) 'Επιτέλους το παραδέχτηκαν: Αποκαλύφθηκε η πραγματική γεύση έχει το πράσινο ζελεδάκι της Haribo', *ENIMEROTIKO*. Available at: www.enimerotiko.gr/plus/epiteloys-to-paradechtikan-apokalyfthike-i-pragmatiki-geysi-echei-to-prasino-zeledaki-tis-haribo/ (Accessed date: 5 December 2023).

Λιάκου, Ε. (2021) *Τεχνικές Ακουστικής Περιγραφής στα Ελληνικά για τον Κινηματογράφο* (Διδακτορική Διατριβή). Τμήμα Ξένων Γλωσσών, Μετάφρασης και Διερμηνείας, Ιόνιο Πανεπιστήμιο. Διαθέσιμο από Εθνικό Αρχείο Διδακτορικών Διατριβών. www.didaktorika.gr/eadd/handle/10442/49679?locale=el

## Filmography

*Το Ταγκό των Χριστουγέννων* (*The Tango of Christmas*), 2011, Νίκος Κουτελιδάκης, N-Orasis Audiovisual.

# 2  Speech acts
## Pinning down communicative intentions

### 2.1  Warm-up

Watch this ad.[1]

- How does non-verbal communication (e.g., setting and props, costumes, kinesics, music, etc.) interact with verbal language in order to convey the overall message?
- What do you think the creators of this advertising campaign intend to communicate with the tagline "Take Pleasure Seriously" (Magnum, 2018)?
- Could this ad work in other cultures or would an adaptation/change of certain features be necessary? Would you opt for a literal or a free translation of the tagline in your native/other working language?

### 2.1  Key concepts

#### 2.1.1  From contextual meaning to force

As explained in Chapter 1, moving from abstract meaning to contextual meaning is the first milestone in the journey that is utterance interpretation. *Contextual meaning* or *utterance meaning* is the first component of *speaker meaning*; the second component of speaker meaning is that of *force*, a term introduced by the philosopher J.L. Austin to describe the speaker's communicative intention (Thomas, 1995: 16–18). Obviously, contextual meaning and force are intimately linked and understanding both of them or neither of them represent the two most likely scenarios in everyday interaction since the former is usually a prerequisite for the latter. However, as Thomas (1995: 21) cautions, the two components of speaker meaning "are not inseparable and it would be a mistake to conflate or confuse them".

How many times have we come across translations that appear accurate but fall short when it comes to capturing and conveying the force of the original communicator?

DOI: 10.4324/9781003213178-3

Speech acts   17

How many times have we misunderstood our interactants because we failed to grasp their communicative intention(s) despite successfully assigning sense and reference in their utterances? In a less likely but still plausible scenario, we may be able to understand force without understanding the meaning of an utterance, for instance, due to an unknown word. In cases like that we tend to rely more on paralinguistic features, nonverbal communication, and/or other contextual information (Thomas, 1995).

To elaborate on the 'understanding utterance meaning but not force' scenario, imagine a colleague says to you, "Did you use real vanilla in there?" In this hypothetical situation, there are no referential ambiguities because the place deictic expression "in there" refers to the cake you have made and brought to work. What about the force of this utterance, though? Is your colleague praising your baking skills? Disapproving of the use of real vanilla because it is quite expensive? Perhaps requesting one more piece of that cake? These are some of the pragmatic forces that this utterance might have. With no help from prosody (e.g., tone of voice, intonation), body language (e.g., facial expression), or background knowledge, it would be very difficult to narrow them down to one and, therefore, the risk of misunderstanding would be fairly high. The aforementioned possibilities, i.e., praising, disapproving, and requesting, respectively, are in fact examples of things that we do with language, also known as *speech acts*, and can be direct or indirect (Yule, 2020). Understanding the speech act performed by the communicator is crucial; if, for instance, an utterance is intended as a request but is interpreted as a disapproval, then that would result in a communicative breakdown (Scott, 2022).

### 2.1.2   Speech act theory

As Cummings (2023: 15) aptly remarks, "the notion that utterances can perform actions may seem quite mundane from today's pragmatically informed standpoint". However, it was quite a revolutionary perspective to adopt amidst the 1950s philosophy of language (ibid). The dominant paradigm back then was that of *Ideal Language Philosophy* which viewed ordinary language as imprecise and vague and, thus, in need of a theory that would render it in a form that would be precise and clear. The *truth conditional theory of meaning* was deemed perfect in this respect since according to its proponents, all we need in order to know the meaning of a sentence is to know the conditions under which that sentence is true (Cummings, 2023). For example, we can assert the truth conditions of the sentence, "The moon orbits the earth". In this light of *logical positivism*, the only meaningful statements are those that can be verified; any statements that cannot be empirically tested are effectively devoid of content and illogical (Thomas, 1995). Effectively, meaning is reduced to truth and language merely to a set of statements describing a state of

## 18    *From abstract meaning to contextual meaning and force*

affairs in the world. It is this reductionist approach to language and the logical positivism of truth conditional semantics that a group of scholars at Oxford and Cambridge, including Austin and Wittgenstein, under the name *Ordinary Language Philosophy* reacted against. To the frustration of Ideal Language Philosophy with the perceived imperfections, ambiguities, and illogicalities of everyday language, J.L. Austin and his group responded by stating the obvious, namely that "people manage to communicate extremely effectively and relatively unproblematically with language just the way it is" (Thomas, 1995: 29). In his very influential collection of papers *How to Do Things With Words* which was published posthumously in 1962, Austin brings into sharp relief that we do not just use language to say things about the world; we also perform actions, thus shaping reality, such as recommending, promising, warning, and challenging as in (a), (b), (c), and (d) respectively:

---

**Example 1**

a) You should aim for 10,000 steps per day.
b) I'll be there as soon as I can, I promise.
c) Sharp scratch!
d) Trick or treat?

---

Austin distinguishes between three different layers or sub-acts in every speech act: the *locution*, i.e. the actual words uttered (or written), the *illocution* or *(illocutionary) force*, i.e., the communicative intention behind the words, and the *perlocution*, i.e., the effect of the locution on the addressee(s) which can take the form of a verbal or a nonverbal reaction (Thomas, 1995: 49). For instance, the locution of (c) would be "sharp scratch" uttered by a nurse before a blood test, the illocution would be that of a warning, and a possible perlocution would be that the patient turns the other way (Desilla, 2019). As far as online communication is concerned, emojis and emoticons accompanying an utterance can help us understand the force of the utterance while a *like* reaction to a post on social media can be regarded as a perlocutionary effect (Scott, 2022). It should be noted that perlocutionary effects are not wholly within the communicator's control; they can be intended or unintended (ibid).

Pinning down the illocution of an utterance is not invariably a foolproof task. As Austin (1962: 99) stresses, "it makes a great difference whether we were advising or merely suggesting, or actually ordering, whether we were strictly promising or only announcing a vague intention and so forth" (cited in Cummings, 2023). He classifies utterances into the following categories depending on their illocution: *verdictives* (e.g., acquitting or convicting someone), *exercitives* (e.g., hiring or firing someone), *commissives* (e.g., vowing or undertaking to do something), *behabitives* (e.g., congratulating, apologising), and *expositives* (e.g., reporting, denying) (ibid). As admitted by

Austin himself, this classification is not without shortcomings. To begin with, *behabitives* is a hold-all term for any utterance pertaining to social behaviour, and, therefore, potentially including a conglomeration of instances. Also, the class of *expositives*, which involves conducting of arguments, expounding of views, or clarifying, has fuzzy boundaries because it may overlap with some of the other classes (Cummings, 2023).

Searle (1979), one of Austin's students at Oxford, proposed his own taxonomy of speech acts addressing some of the weaknesses of Austin's classification:

*Table 2.1.2* Searle's (1979) classification of speech acts

| Speech Act Types | Description | Examples |
|---|---|---|
| Assertives | Expressing belief/committing to something being the case | • stating<br>• predicting<br>• affirming<br>• claiming<br>• blaming |
| Directives | Attempting to get the hearer to do something | • ordering<br>• requesting<br>• challenging<br>• begging<br>• suggesting |
| Commissives | Committing to a future action | • promising<br>• vowing<br>• refusing<br>• accepting<br>• threatening |
| Expressives | Expressing a psychological state about a state of affairs | • congratulating<br>• apologising<br>• condoling<br>• praising<br>• complimenting |
| Declaratives | Changing reality according to the locution | • firing<br>• pronouncing<br>• declaring<br>• denouncing<br>• christening |

Searle further developed Speech Act Theory in yet another way: his account of *indirect speech acts* (1975; 1979) sheds more light on how "the game of illocutionary acts" (Searle, 1969: 55) is played. Consider the two images in Example 2. The images are photographs of both sides of an actual sign on Livadi Beach on the Greek island of Irakleia, which belongs to Minor Cyclades in the heart of the Aegean Archipelago. Image (a) shows the sign in Greek while its English version can be seen in image (b). The target-text (TT), i.e., "Got your phone? Your wallet? Your trash?" is a verbatim translation of

## Example 2

*Speech acts* 21

the original. In all probability, the communicator here is not really interested in receiving an actual answer to these questions. The interrogative structure is used here to perform a function other than a question (cf. Yule, 2020). This is an example of an *indirect speech act*. According to Searle (1979: 31), an indirect speech act emerges when "one illocutionary act is performed indirectly by way of performing another". This is an intriguing phenomenon demonstrating that communication can still be smooth despite communicative intentions being opaque and will be discussed in more depth in Chapter 3. In the case of the beach sign, the indirect speech act is that of a *directive* and more specifically a request that visitors take all their belongings with them, and importantly, their trash when leaving the beach. Arguably, the sign first and foremost conveys a request to keep the beach clean. The reference to the phone and wallet can be regarded rather as an attention-getting device paving the way to the core of the message. Valuables such as our mobile phone and wallet are usually among the first things that we check when leaving a place; personal waste is often left behind.

Although in the beach sign example the English TT successfully conveys the illocution of the original, and through preserving the indirect nature of the speech act intact, for that matter, handling speech acts in translation is not always a straightforward process. Hatim and Mason (1997), who were among the first scholars in translation studies to show interest in the handling of pragmatic meaning, found that there may be shifts from indirect to direct speech acts in film subtitling owing to physical constraints intrinsic to this mode of AVT. For instance, an indirect request expressed by means of an interrogative structure which contains some hedging, i.e., "Could you perhaps give me a ride to the airport tonight, please?" may be rendered as, "Please, give me a ride to the airport tonight" due to limitations of time and/or space. The evidently shorter subtitled version uses an imperative structure that might make the on-screen character come across as less polite or more abrupt. Therefore, shifts in the structure of the utterance which also include omissions of indicators of modality need to be undertaken with caution (Díaz-Cintas & Remael, 2021).

Moving on to a revoicing mode of AVT, that of dubbing, let us examine the following speech act:

---

**Example 3**

ST: Should I make your pulse rise? Or . . . stop!
TT1: Θα κάνω την καρδιά σου να χτυπάει δυνατά. Ἡ μήπως . . . καθόλου.
BT1: I'm going to make your heart beat fast. Or perhaps, not at all?
TT2: Posso farti battere il cuore . . . oppure . . . posso fermarlo.
BT2: I can make your heart beat . . . or . . . I can stop it.

(PucsRes, 2014)

## 22  *From abstract meaning to contextual meaning and force*

The utterance in question belongs to Ahri who is a videogame character in *League of Legends. League of Legends* (*LoL*) is a free-to-play multiplayer online battle arena (MOBA) videogame developed and published by Riot Games. Released in 2009, *LoL* has been localised into 20 different languages and has been immensely popular across cultures. Ahri is among the 150 plus available champions, i.e., characters that players can choose and control during a battle in *LoL*. Ahri "can manipulate her prey's emotions and consume their essence – receiving flashes of their memory and insight from each soul she consumes" (*League of Legends*, 2009). In this instance, "Should I make your pulse rise? Or . . . stop!" is one of Ahri's *taunts*, a term which in the context of videogames refers to "a sarcastic remark, gesture, or insult by which gamers deliberately demoralize or anger their opponents (primarily to make them act in a haste and hence cause them to make mistakes)" (Balogh & Veszelszki, 2020: 74). On this basis, taunts can be thought of as belonging to the directive speech act type since they are provocative in nature aiming at eliciting a response from the addressee. The English original initially comes in the form of a question "should I make your pulse rise?" but then the intonation falls ("Or . . . stop!"). In both the Greek and the Italian translations there is a shift from the interrogative structure to the declarative structure, with the intonation of the Greek voice talent rising in the second part (PucsRes, 2014). In addition, the word *heart* (καρδιά/cuore) has been used instead of *pulse* which can be considered a successful modulation (Vinay & Darbelnet, 1958/1977). Nevertheless, it is the shift in structure as well as lexical choices of "θα κάνω" in TT1 and "posso farti . . . posso fermarlo" in TT2 that result in a different speech act type and an ever so slightly different style. The indirect speech act of the original is that of a challenge/provocation with some threatening undertones. However, the element of the threat is more prominent in the Greek version which can be thought of as illustrating a commissive speech act type, at least at first glance, while the Italian version seems more like an assertion again with some threatening undertones, stating what Ahri is capable of doing. Interestingly enough, both TT1 and TT2 perform the illocution of a provocation (indirect speech act) but through performing two different illocutions on a surface level. Because "gaming is experienced through both illocutionary and perlocutionary acts" (Colăcel, 2017: 43), pragmatic meaning should be given due attention in videogame localisation (cf. Bernal-Merino, 2016).

Apart from genre-specific considerations and mode-specific constraints, an additional factor that may affect the treatment of speech acts in translation pertains to cross-cultural pragmatic differences. Although most speech acts appear to be universal, the way they are realised by source and target cultures may vary (Bruti, 2019). For example, while speakers tend to use imperatives when offering advice in Polish, more indirect and hedged forms are preferred in English (Wierzbicka, 1991/2003). In a similar vein, direct requests which are perfectly normal in Italian might come across as impolite

*Speech acts* 23

if literally translated into English (Katan, 2002). Compliments comprise another "culturally-constrained speech act", as reported by Bruti (2006, 2009, 2014).

## 2.2 Case study

Advertising translation is another area where the application of pragmatics and, in particular, speech act theory, can be beneficial both from a research as well as a professional practice perspective (Valdés, 2019). As Valdés explains, in ads "utterances are generally used to perform the act of persuasion and to enact an effect of consumption" (2019: 180). The translator here can take liberties with the text, e.g., changing speech acts from assertive to directive or the other way around, as long as the overall *persuasive/operative function* (Reiss, 1976/1989) is maintained across cultures (Trosborg, 1997; Valdés, 2019). Of course, pragmatic meaning in ads works very often in tandem with non-verbal signifiers. Audiovisual ads are *par excellence* multimodal texts. According to Baldry and Thibault (2006: 18), "multimodal texts are *composite* products of the combined effect of all the resources used to create and interpret them".

The Magnum ice cream ad (Magnum, 2018) included in the warm-up exercise is an excellent case in point. This commercial, part of the "Take Pleasure Seriously" campaign produced by advertising agency LOLA MullenLowe, wields the power of an impressive amount of semiotic resources carefully orchestrated to create the effect of a Roaring Twenties party atmosphere and hedonistic indulgence (Glasnost, n.d., online). The target audience is mainly Millennials and the goal is to communicate the idea of "serious pleasure" while linking it to the brand and the premium ingredients in Magnum ice cream (ibid). Apart from the opulent and extravagant *mise-en-scène* (the majestic mansion setting, the penguins, the dancers' costumes and protagonist's gold dress, the bespoke ice cream wooden stick, the golden confetti at the end, etc.), the creators have deftly employed several *types of nonverbal communication* (Jackson, 2014) to this end, such as *kinesics* (e.g., the penguin-like walking, the dancing, the smiles), *proxemics* (e.g., the intimate distance between the female protagonist and the Magnum ingredients), and *oculesics* (the knowing looks exchanged with the Belgian chocolatier/mixologist, her intense gaze through the periscope-shaker contraption). To this multisensorial experience one should add the jazz song dominating the soundtrack until the voice-over talks us through the high-quality ingredients of the ice cream and is concluded by the tagline "Take Pleasure Seriously", which also features as a verbal-visual element against a rain of golden confetti.

When it comes to international marketing campaigns, there are two main approaches, namely *standardisation* and *localisation* (Torresi, 2021): standardisation is based on the assumption that consumers everywhere have

## 24  *From abstract meaning to contextual meaning and force*

similar wants and needs; thus, there is a single advertising message that travels globally with minor modifications (e.g., translations of slogans, taglines). In localisation, on the other hand, the message is tailored to the preferences and needs of individual countries. Localisation often involves *transcreation* which can be defined as "a type of adaptation that involves copywriting [i.e. developing the verbal part of the ad] and possibly prompting the creation of new visuals for the promotional material rather than relying on the same verbal and visual structure of the source text" (Torresi, 2021: 199). Magnum's 'Take Pleasure Seriously' was a global campaign, and, indeed, the Greek version of the commercial (Magic Ice Cream, 2018) evidences a standardisation approach, overall:

ST: Take pleasure seriously.
TT: Πάρτε σοβαρά την απόλαυση. BT: Take [plural] seriously the pleasure.

As can be seen, the tagline in the voice over has been literally translated into Greek, preserving the directive speech act as well as the imperative construction. The grammatical form of the Greek verb, however, is in the second person plural addressing the audience collectively. This translation decision is in line with the traditional genre conventions of Greek advertising (Sidiropoulou, 1998). The second person singular, embedded in this imperative construction, might have come across as too direct and/or imposing; having said that, it is a stylistic choice that has begun to infiltrate Greek audiovisual ads over the last few years. It is noteworthy that the Greek commercial (Magic Ice Cream, 2018) is a much shorter version of the English original (Magnum, 2018) and features the brand name *Magic* instead of *Magnum* since the latter is an ice cream brand owned by another company in Greece.

Although as Trosborg (1997) points out, the aim in advertising translation is "not necessarily matching speech act to speech act"; in this case retaining the directive in the TT serves the purpose and the intended perlocutionary effects quite well. We should also bear in mind that translators more often than not work with specific briefs which include rather strict guidelines from marketing teams regarding what can and cannot be changed in the target versions (Torresi, 2021).

### 2.3  Exercises and mini research activities

1) Look for any target versions of the Magnum (2018) ad in your other working languages.

   - How is the tagline translated? Is the directive speech act type preserved in the TT? Are there any changes in the visuals?
   - If you can find no versions or if the versions found are similar to the Greek version analysed in the case study, try to come up with a more creative translation which would also illustrate a change from the

directive to an assertive speech act. Make sure that your version still serves the purpose of the original campaign.

2) Choose your favourite film/series/videogame accessible both in English and in one of your other working languages. Focus on a short excerpt (e.g., 10–15 min.) and make a list of any speech acts identified along with their types following Searle's (1979) taxonomy. Then compare them to their subtitled or dubbed versions. Can you observe any shifts? If so, try to reflect on the possible rationale underlying the translator's choices.

## 2.4 Suggestions for further reading

*On speech acts:*

Austin, J.L. (1962) *How to Do Things with Words*, Oxford: Oxford University Press.
Cummings, L. (2023) *Introducing Pragmatics: A Clinical Approach*, Oxon and New York: Routledge, Chapter 1.
Searle, J.R. (1979) *Expression and Meaning: Studies in the Theory of Speech Acts*, Cambridge: Cambridge University Press.
Thomas, J. (1995) *Meaning in Interaction. An Introduction to Pragmatics*, London: Longman, Chapter 2.
Wierzbicka, A. (1991/2003) *Cross-Cultural Pragmatics: The Semantics of Human Interaction*, Berlin and New York: Mouton de Gruyter, Chapters 2 and 5.

*On speech acts and translation:*

Bonsignori, V., & Bruti, S. (2015) 'Conversational Routines Across Languages: The Case of Leavetakings and Greetings in Original and Dubbed Films', in J. Díaz Cintas & J. Neves (eds.), *Audiovisual Translation: Taking Stock*, Newcastle upon Tyne: Cambridge Scholars Publishing, 28–45.
Bourne, J. (2002) 'He Said, She Said: Controlling Illocutionary Force in the Translation of Literary Dialogue', *Target* 14(2): 241–261.
Bruti, S. (2006) 'Cross-cultural Pragmatics: The Translation of Implicit Compliments in Subtitles', *JoSTrans: The Journal of Specialised Translation* 6: 185–197. Available at: www.jostrans.org/issue06/art_bruti.php (Accessed date: 4 December 2023).
Bruti, S. (2019) 'Speech Acts and Translation', in R. Tipton & L. Desilla (eds.), *The Routledge Handbook of Translation and Pragmatics*, Oxon and New York: Routledge, 13–26.
Hervey, S.G.J. (1998) 'Speech Acts and Illocutionary Function in Translation Methodology', in L. Hickey (ed.), *The Pragmatics of Translation*, Clevedon: Multilingual Matters, 54–71.
Katan, D. (2002) 'Mediating the Point of Refraction and Playing with the Perlocutionary Effect: A Translator's Choice?', in S. Herbrechter (ed.), *Cultural Studies: Interdisciplinarity and Translation*, Amsterdam and New York: Rodopi, 177–195.
Pedersen, J. (2008) 'High Felicity: A Speech Act Approach to Quality Assessment in Subtitling', in D. Chiaro, C. Heiss & C. Bucaria (eds.), *Between Text and Image: Updating Research in Screen Translation*, Amsterdam and Philadelphia: John Benjamins, 101–115.
Polcz, K. (2020) *Speech Acts, Directness and Politeness in Dubbing*. American Television Series in Hungary, Oxford: Peter Lang.

## Note

1  https://www.youtube.com/watch?v=8BJkVKxmi68

## References

Austin, J.L. (1962) *How to Do Things with Words*, Oxford: Oxford University Press.

Baldry, A., & Thibault, P. (2006) *Multimodal Transcription and Text Analysis. A Multimodal Toolkit and Coursebook*, London: Equinox.

Balogh, A., & Veszelszki, A. (2020) 'Politeness and Insult in Computer Games – From a Pragmatic Point of View', *Acta Universitatis Sapientiae, Communicatio* 7: 68–91.

Bernal-Merino, M. (2016) 'Creating Felicitous Gaming Experiences: Semiotics and Pragmatics as Tools for Video Game Localisation', *Signata* 7: 231–253. https://doi.org/10.4000/signata.1227

Bruti, S. (2006) 'Cross-cultural Pragmatics: The Translation of Implicit Compliments in Subtitles', *JoSTrans: The Journal of Specialised Translation* 6: 185–197. Available at: www.jostrans.org/issue06/art_bruti.php (Accessed date: 4 December 2023).

Bruti, S. (2009) 'Translating Compliments in Subtitles', in A. Baldry, M. Pavesi, C. Taylor Toresello & C. Taylor (eds.), *From Didactas to Ecolingua: An Ongoing Research Project on Translation and Corpus Linguistics*, Trieste: Edizioni Università di Trieste, 91–110.

Bruti, S. (2014) 'Compliments in Fansubs and in Professional Subtitles: The Case of Lost', *Rivista Internazionale di Technica della Traduzione (International Journal of Translation)* 16: 13–34.

Bruti, S. (2019) 'Speech Acts and Translation', in R. Tipton & L. Desilla (eds.), *The Routledge Handbook of Translation and Pragmatics*, Oxon and New York: Routledge, 13–26.

Colăcel, O. (2017) 'Speech Acts in Post-Apocalyptic Games: The Last of Us (2014)', *Messages, Sages and Ages* 4(1): 41–50. https://doi.org/10.1515/msas-2017-0004

Cummings, L. (2023) *Introducing Pragmatics: A Clinical Approach*, Oxon and New York: Routledge.

Desilla, L. (2019) 'Pragmatics', in L. Pérez González (ed.), *The Routledge Handbook of Audiovisual Translation Studies*, Oxon and New York: Routledge, 242–258.

Díaz-Cintas, J., & Remael, A. (2021) *Subtitling: Concepts and Practices*, Oxon and New York: Routledge.

Glasnost (n.d.) *A Night at the Magnum Mansion*. Available at: https://glasnost.amsterdam/en/work/a-night-at-the-magnum-mansion/ (Accessed date: 4 December 2023).

Hatim, B., & Mason, I. (1997) *The Translator as Communicator*, London and New York: Longman.

Jackson, J. (2014) *Introducing Language and Intercultural Communication*, Oxon and New York: Routledge.

Katan, D. (2002) 'Mediating the Point of Refraction and Playing with the Perlocutionary Effect: A Translator's Choice?', in S. Herbrechter (ed.), *Cultural Studies: Interdisciplinarity and Translation*, Amsterdam and New York: Rodopi, 177–195.

Magic Ice Cream (2018) *Magic – Πάρτε την Απόλαυση στα Σοβαρά* [Video]. Available at: www.youtube.com/watch?v=9nQLuklbsr4 (Accessed date: 4 December 2023).

Magnum (2018) *Magnum Classic – Take Pleasure Seriously* [Video]. Available at: www.youtube.com/watch?v=emHXiF3Cb_g (Accessed date: 4 December 2023).

PucsRes (2014) *LoL Voices – Ahri- In 17 Languages* [Video]. YouTube. Available at: www.youtube.com/watch?v=T4ohzAPxC8o (Accessed date: 4 December 2023).

Reiss, K. (1976/1989) 'Text Types, Translation Types and Translation Assessment', in A. Chesterman (ed.), *Readings in Translation Theory*, Helsinki: Oy Finn Lectura.

Scott, K. (2022) *Pragmatics Online*, Oxon and New York: Routledge.
Searle, J.R. (1969) *Speech Acts: An Essay in the Philosophy of Language*, Cambridge: Cambridge University Press.
Searle, J.R. (1975) 'Indirect Speech Acts', in P. Cole & J. Morgan (eds.), *Syntax and Semantics 3: Speech Acts*, New York: Academic, 59–82.
Searle, J.R. (1979) *Expression and Meaning: Studies in the Theory of Speech Acts*, Cambridge: Cambridge University Press.
Sidiropoulou, M. (1998) 'Advertising in Translation: English vs. Greek', *Meta* 43(2): 191–204. https://doi.org/10.7202/004141ar
Thomas, J. (1995) *Meaning in Interaction. An Introduction to Pragmatics*, London: Longman.
Torresi, I. (2021) *Translating Promotional and Advertising Texts*. 2nd edition, Oxon and New York: Routledge.
Trosborg, A. (1997) 'Text Typology: Register, Genre and Text-Type', in A. Trosborg (ed.), *Text Typology and Translation*, Amsterdam and Philadelphia: John Benjamins, 3–24.
Valdés, C. (2019) 'Advertising Translation and Pragmatics', in R. Tipton & L. Desilla (eds.), *The Routledge Handbook of Translation and Pragmatics*, Oxon and New York: Routledge, 171–190.
Vinay, J.P., & Darbelnet, J. (1958/1977) *Stylistique Comparee du Francais et l'Anglais: Methode de Traduction*, Paris: Didier. Translated and edited by J. Sager & M.J. Hamel (1995) as *Comparative Stylistics of French and English: A Methodology for Translation*, Amsterdam and Philadelphia: John Benjamins.
Wierzbicka, A. (1991/2003) *Cross-Cultural Pragmatics: The Semantics of Human Interaction*, Berlin and New York: Mouton de Gruyter.
Yule, G. (2020) *The Study of Language*. 7th edition, New York: Cambridge University Press.

*Gameography*

League of Legends (2009) *Riot Games*. Available at: https://www.leagueoflegends.com/en-us/

Part II

# Navigating interpersonal meaning and communicative styles

# 3 Implicature
## Reading between the lines

## 3.1 Warm-up

Have a look at the following meme tokens belonging to the *Baby Yoda Meme* family:

a) Baby Yoda Cookies Meme 1 (2021)[1]

[Website: "We use cookies to improve performance"
Me: Same]

b) Baby Yoda Cookies Meme 2 (n.d.)[2]

[When you click "accept cookies" and then you don't get any cookies]

Try to translate the bracketed verbal component of the two memes into one of your native/foreign languages and make a note of any challenges faced.

## 3.2 Key concepts

### 3.2.1 *The salience of linguistic indirectness*

As demonstrated in Chapter 2, the comprehension of utterance meaning is not always straightforward; very often, communicators mean much more than what they actually utter (Levinson, 1983). Opaque or indirect meaning appears to be universal; it is observable in all natural languages and potentially in any environment where language is used as one of the means for communication (Thomas, 1995). Before we embark upon the two main theoretical approaches to implicature, it would be helpful to cast a glance at the key features of linguistic indirectness, in general, namely *conscious intentionality* and *high risk*, as well as the rather intriguing link between the two.

Although the ability to use and understand indirect meaning may be compromised by neurodevelopmental disorders, psychiatric conditions, or brain injury (Cummings, 2023), within mainstream pragmatic enquiry, linguistic indirectness usually entails what Verschueren (1999: 31) refers to as "strategic avoidance of explicitness". In other words, we are not interested in

DOI: 10.4324/9781003213178-5

## 32 *Navigating interpersonal meaning and communicative styles*

indirectness which occurs due to an inability to say something explicitly but rather in the communicators' conscious and deliberate choice to exploit lack of verbal transparency in order to achieve their communicative goals (Dascal, 1983; Thomas, 1995). Accordingly, addressees interpret an utterance as indirect if they assume that there is a viable reason to look beyond its locution (Dascal, 2003). Besides, indirectness is a costly and risky mode of communication; it requires a greater amount of cognitive effort on the addressee's part while increasing the likelihood of the illocutionary force being misunderstood or altogether impenetrable (Weizman, 1989: 73; cf. Dascal, 1983).

But if the sheer presence of indirectness substantially raises the utterance comprehension stakes so much, why is it our preferred choice in several communicative situations? The answer to this question invariably resides in one or more of its rewards (Lee & Pinker, 2010). Importantly, indirectness can make one's language more interesting/appealing, maximise the impact of one's message, and/or serve as a face-saving strategy (Thomas, 1995: 142–146). Since the latter falls under *politeness*, it is explained in Chapter 4. The first two advantages seem to be intimately linked with one another. For instance, wordplays as well as figures of speech, such as metaphor and irony, intrinsically involve indirect meaning and can contribute to a more evocative, creative, engaging, and/or playful style, thus reinforcing the effectiveness of one's message (Thomas, 1995). As Tannen points out (1989: 23), by inviting the addressee "to fill in unstated meaning, indirectness contributes to a sense of involvement through mutual participation in sense making". At the same time, indirectness can minimise distance between interactants; in essence, the communicator makes a claim of common ground since s/he expects to be understood merely by evoking information assumed to be shared with the addressee(s) (ibid; Mooney, 2004; Terkourafi, 2011). Therefore, indirectness can be used to construe intimacy or the illusion thereof, the latter often referred to as *pseudo-intimacy* or *false intimacy* by media discourse scholars (Durant & Lambrou, 2009; cf. Hoggart, 1957; Goffman, 1981). It is no surprise then that implicit meaning is observable not only in real, interpersonal communication (face-to-face or computer-mediated but also in fictional communication (Kozloff, 2000; Desilla, 2012), as well as in media communication genres, such as advertisements (Torresi, 2021; Valdés, 2019) and memes (Scott, 2022). What is more, the very fact that that translation allows, at least in theory, for the opportunity to make changes along the directness-indirectness continuum, thus potentially tampering with pragmatic meaning as intended by the source-language (SL) communicator(s), renders cross-cultural explorations of implicature particularly insightful.

### 3.2.2 *The Gricean approach to implicature*

Grice's work on implicature is the first systematic attempt to elucidate the phenomenon whereby speakers mean more than what is linguistically encoded in their utterances, a layer of meaning which, as shown in Part I of this book,

*Implicature* 33

cannot be satisfactorily accounted for by semantics alone. Grice was the first to coin the term *implicate* along with its derivatives *implicature* and *implicatum*[3] (1975/1991: 305–306).

It has been claimed that the most significant component of the Gricean heritage is its fresh approach to meaning (Avramides, 1989; Chapman, 2005: 90). Its originality resides mainly in the specification of meaning in terms of speaker intentions and in the view of meaning as a heterogeneous, composite concept. In particular, the construal of *non-natural meaning* appears as the founding stone of Grice's theory of conversation and implicature (Marmaridou, 2000: 26). According to Grice, there are two distinct senses in which the term *mean* may be used (1957: 377). The following utterances demonstrate these uses:

---

**Example 1**

a) Love means kindness and care (BBC Teach, n.d.).
b) "I'm fine" means "I'm falling apart and I need your help" (The Depression Project, n.d.).

---

The first utterance is actually one of the responses of primary school pupils when asked what love means to them, available on the BBC Teach website. Here the lexical item "means" could be replaced with "entails", whereas in the second utterance this is not feasible. In other words, "I'm falling apart and I need your help" is not an entailment of "I'm fine", since the truth of the former does not follow from the truth of the latter. As *The Depression Project* mental health organisation reports, this is what sometimes people with depression mean when they say "I'm fine" for a variety of reasons. To cater for these two different uses of *mean*, Grice distinguishes between what he, rather idiosyncratically, calls *natural meaning*, as illustrated in (1), and *non-natural meaning* or *meaning*$_{nn}$, as exemplified in (2) (1957: 378–379).

*Intentionality* in communication is a crucial notion for Grice because each utterance is intended to create an effect upon the recipient (ibid: 383). Not only that; the speaker wants the addressee to recognise that this effect was indeed intended and not accidental (ibid). More precisely, communication involves "a complex, reflexive intention" (Levinson, 2000: 13; Marmaridou, 2000: 226). Since intention is a cognitive phenomenon, speaker meaning is here defined in psychological terms (Chapman, 2005: 66). Grice has been both praised and criticised for this novelty (ibid: 63–66).

The second important facet of the "Gricean umbrella" is the argument that meaning$_{nn}$ is not uniform but complex and multi-layered (Levinson, 2000: 13).

Put differently, meaning consists of various sub-levels rather than being a homogeneous whole (ibid). Grice draws a primary distinction between two layers of meaning, namely *what is said* and *what is implicated* (ibid). Figure 3.2.2 designates the Gricean 'dissection' of utterance meaning:

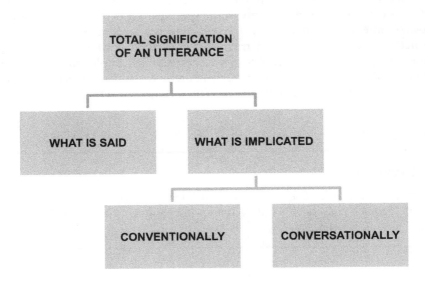

*Figure 3.2.2* Layers of meaning
Source: Adapted from Levinson (2000: 13)

On the one hand, linguistically encoded meaning encompasses what is said and what is conventionally implicated (Levinson, 2000: 14). On the other hand, what is conversationally implicated is not a part of the truth-conditional content of the utterance, but is recovered via an inferential process (ibid) which is explained subsequently.

*Types and properties of implicature*

The fundamentals of Grice's approach to conversation and implicature can be found in his seminal publication entitled "Logic and Conversation" (1975), which is based on one of his University of Harvard lectures given in 1967 (Atlas, 2005: 45). As evidenced by the titular juxtaposition, conversation is viewed here as rational behaviour. More precisely, Grice argues that interactions are anything but haphazard; they are co-operative, rule-governed exchanges (1975/1991). With respect to co-operation, in particular, interlocutors are assumed to expect and show some helpfulness in pursuing certain communicative goals (Chapman, 2005: 98). This rational, co-operative, and goal-oriented nature of communication is encapsulated in Grice's

*Implicature* 35

*Cooperative Principle* and the four maxims of conversation, namely Quality, Quantity, Relation, and Manner:

Cooperative Principle: Make your conversational contribution such as is required, at the stage at which it occurs, by the accepted purpose or direction of the talk exchange in which you are engaged.

(Grice, 1975/1991: 307)

*Table 3.2.2* The Gricean Maxims of Conversation (Grice, 1975/1991: 308–309)

| Maxims of Conversation | Specifications |
|---|---|
| Quantity | • Make your contribution as informative as is required (for the current purposes of the exchange). |
| | • Do not make your contribution more informative than is required. |
| Quality | • Do not say what you believe to be false. |
| | • Do not say that for which you lack adequate evidence. |
| Relation | • Be relevant. |
| Manner | • Avoid obscurity. |
| | • Avoid ambiguity. |
| | • Be brief. |
| | • Be orderly. |

As Grice stresses, although people often fail to observe the maxims of conversation, presented in Table 3.2.2, communication can still be successful as it unfolds based on the premise that (at least) the CP is adhered to at all times (cf., Marmaridou, 2000: 229–230). Maxim non-observance can take different forms[4]; however, the generation of conversational implicatures is exclusive to maxim *floutings* or *exploitations*, whereby communicators strategically choose not to observe a maxim in order to obtain a communicative advantage (Grice, 1975/1991: 310). But exactly how do conversational implicatures emerge in such a framework?

Before addressing this question, we need to consider the kinds of implied meaning identified by Grice. He was very concerned with demonstrating the difference between two ways of implying. In his own words, "[The focus is on the] radical importance of distinguishing (to speak loosely) what *our words* say or imply from what *we* in uttering them imply" (Grice, 1986: 69; emphasis in original). A primary distinction is drawn between *conventional implicature* and *conversational implicature*. Conventional implicatures are described as heavily dependent on linguistic meaning and not on the context of utterance (Grice, 1975/1991: 306–307). For instance, compare and contrast "Meg is a diligent student but not a nerd" to "Meg is a diligent student and not a nerd". The first utterance is indicative of the implicatures conventionally triggered by the word *but*. The implicature here is that diligent

## 36  *Navigating interpersonal meaning and communicative styles*

students are stereotypically considered nerds. This implicature, however, is not conveyed by the second utterance. Both assert the same state of affairs, thus sharing the same truth-conditional content. Yet, the use of "but" suggests a contradiction in Meg being a diligent student and simultaneously not being a nerd.

To conventional implicature Grice juxtaposes conversational implicature. As Thomas observes, their similarity resides in that "they both convey an additional level of meaning beyond the semantic meaning of the words uttered" (1995: 57). However, their point of divergence lies in that conversational implicatures are, to a greater or a lesser extent, inextricably linked with the context of utterance. In conventional implicatures, by contrast, the same implicature is always expressed irrespective of the particular occasion on which an utterance occurs (ibid). Besides, Grice stresses that conversational implicatures are related to specific discourse features, namely the CP and the four maxims (1975/1991: 313) and that it is essential that conversational implicatures "are capable of being worked out" and not merely "intuitively grasped" (ibid, 1975/1991: 312–313). Otherwise, the implicature is considered conventional (ibid). Conversational implicatures are further subdivided into *generalised conversational implicatures* and *particularised conversational implicatures* (Grice, 1975/1991). The acronyms GCIs and PCIs have been proposed by Levinson (2000: 16) and will be used henceforth.

In an attempt to illustrate GCIs, Grice juxtaposes the utterance "Luke is meeting *a* woman this evening" to "I broke *a* finger yesterday" (Grice, 1975/1991: 314; emphasis added). Regardless of particular circumstances, the first utterance implies that in all probability Luke is not meeting his wife, close friend, or a female sibling for that matter. If that were the case, the speaker would be expected to have said so clearly, since he is assumed to observe the CP and the maxim of Manner. In this light, and given that there is no specific contextual information pointing towards a different interpretation, the addressee is to infer that the woman Luke is about to meet is not a very close acquaintance. As Marmaridou points out, such implicatures pertaining to the "alienation of an object from an agent" are frequently activated by the use of the article "a" (2000: 234). However, as the second utterance indicates, this is not always the case. Therefore, these 'alienation implicatures' cannot be regarded as a semantic or pragmatic feature of the indefinite article *per se* (ibid). The article "a" in the second utterance does not convey any implication of that kind. Quite the contrary; it is to be inferred that the finger the speaker is referring to is actually his/her own (Grice, 1975/1991: 314). The implicatures exemplified by the two utterances are both GCIs and, thus, differentiated from conventional implicatures, which emerge from the use of certain lexical items as an intrinsic part of their meaning (Marmaridou, 2000: 235).

In the remainder of this section, the focus will be exclusively on PCIs, which are triggered by maxim floutings (Grice, 1975/1991: 310). This type

*Implicature* 37

of conversational implicature always arises in a particular context, hence the term *particularised* (Levinson, 1983: 126). PCIs can be illustrated by means of the following dialogue[5]:

---

**Example 2**

[*This talk exchange takes place at a club in central London. The inter-locutors have just met. A confident Jack makes advances at Alice whose body languages suggests lack of interest.*]

Jack: So, your place or mine?
Alice: I'd rather eat a Galaxy.

---

Jack's utterance is an indirect invitation for Alice to spend the night with him (Desilla, 2019b: 249–250). At first glance, Alice's response seems completely irrelevant and rather obscure thus flouting the maxim of Relation and possibly also Manner. Still, according to Grice, we have to assume that Alice observes the CP. To be able to maintain this assumption and decipher Alice's utterance, Jack needs to activate his background knowledge and, more specifically that (a) Galaxy is a chocolate bar marketed in the UK and crucially (b) chocolate is considered a substitute for sexual pleasure. It is only by recalling and combining these two pieces of information that Jack is able to fully recover what Alice communicates in an implicit yet quite derisive manner indeed, namely that she does not fancy him at all. Importantly, Alice assumes that this knowledge is accessible by Jack. The availability of such relevant items to the addressee(s) is a *sine qua non* in working out implicatures. As Baker (2011: 259) demonstrates, "translators often find themselves in the position of having to reassess what is and what is not available to target readers to ensure that implicatures can be worked out". Some food for thought then: if the exchange between Jack and Alice were actually a film dialogue excerpt, how would a subtitler handle Alice's response in a hypothetical scenario where Galaxy chocolates are not marketed in the target culture?

Another possibility is to overtly flout maxims in order to produce figures of speech like metaphor, irony, overstatement, and understatement (Grice, 1975/1991: 312). Thus, metaphoric, ironic, hyperbolic, and meiotic expressions are regarded as generating PCIs, the first two by exploiting the Quality maxim while the latter by exploiting the Quantity maxim (ibid; Cummings, 2023: 43–44). Consider the following excerpt from *Finding Nemo* (2003) along with its subtitled (TT1) and dubbed (TT2) DVD versions (Stanton & Unkrich, 2004) into Greek (Desilla, 2005):

# 38 *Navigating interpersonal meaning and communicative styles*

---

**Example 3**

**ST:**   (DENTIST) All right, let's see those pearly whites.
(DARLA) Raaah: I'm a piranha! They're in the Amazon.

**TT1:** Λοιπόν, για να δούμε/τα μαργαριταράκια σου.
Είμαι πιράνχας. Ζουν στον Αμαζόνιο.

**BT1:** So, let's see your pearls [diminutive].
I'm a piranha. They live in the Amazon.

**TT2:** Εντάξει. Για να δούμε τα δόντια σου.
Είμαι πιράνχα! Εκεί στον Αμαζόνιο.

**BT2:** All right. Let's see your teeth.
I'm a piranha. There, in the Amazon.

---

In this scene fragment, an overexcited 8-year-old Darla, wearing braces with orthodontic headgear, sits on the dentist's chair. When she exclaims "I'm a piranha!" having just attempted to bite the dentist's index finger, she flouts the first sub-maxim of Quality, i.e., that of truthfulness, presumably in order to implicitly communicate how sharp her teeth are. The piranha metaphor is preserved intact in both TT1 and TT2. It is noteworthy that the subtitled version features a metaphor which is not expressed in the ST as such: "pearly whites" has been rendered as "pearls [diminutive]" (i.e., little pearls) which still evokes the image of clean, white, sparkly teeth albeit in a more original and less direct manner. Despite this minor modification, it can be claimed that both TT1 and TT2 are *pragmatically equivalent* (Baker, 2011) to the original dialogue.

Floutings which lead to figurative language, like the example, are called maxim exploitations (Levinson, 1983: 109). Whether emerging from simple maxim floutings or exploitations, PCIs can be worked out via an inferential process (Grice, 1975/1991: 315). Put differently, PCIs are *calculable* (ibid). Levinson (1983: 113–114), based on Grice, has formulated the following schema, designating the successive steps of the reasoning process for the calculation of the implicature $q$:

(i)   S has said that $p$

(ii)  there is no reason to think S is not observing the maxims or at least the co-operative principle

(iii) in order for S to say that $p$ and indeed observing the maxims or the co-operative principle, S must think that $q$

(iv) S must know that it is mutual knowledge that $q$ must be supposed if S is to be taken to be co-operating

(v)  S has done nothing to stop me, the addressee, thinking that $q$

(vi) therefore S intends me to think that $q$, and in saying that $p$ has implicated $q$

*Implicature* 39

Apart from calculability, Grice recognises another key property of conversational implicatures, namely that of *indeterminacy* (Grice, 1975: 315). Since a single instance of implicature may elicit a range of different interpretations, the conversational implicatum of an utterance cannot be precisely specified at all times (ibid). In discussing the elusive and fluid nature of PCIs, Thomas stresses that "implicatures are the property of *utterances*, not of sentences and therefore the same words [may well] carry different implicatures on different occasions" (1995: 80; emphasis added). Baker (2011: 238), who illuminates the link between implicatures and coherence, underscores that implicature indeterminacy and open-endedness "complicate the task of the translator who may knowingly or unknowingly eliminate certain possible interpretations of the original text . . . or may even inadvertently give rise to other interpretations" which were not originally intended.

### Mini discussion of Gricean theory

Grice's theory of communication, in general, and implicature, in particular has left its hallmark in the field (Recanati, 1991: 97; Wilson, 1994: 55). The recognition of meaning as a heterogeneous, multi-layered concept is considered a major advance in semantics and pragmatics (Levinson, 2000: 21). Furthermore, the definition of meaning from a psychological perspective in terms of speaker intentions remains another innovation irrespective of the criticisms it has attracted (Verschueren, 1999: 47; Chapman, 2005: 63–66). Grice's most important legacy is perhaps the approach to conversational implicature, a phenomenon apparently ignored by his contemporary linguists and philosophers of language. Notwithstanding the weaknesses discussed below, the Gricean framework shows that the recovery of conversational implicatures requires an inferential mechanism, a reasoning process with successive steps in which certain conversational principles play a decisive, structural role. The CP and maxims of conversation can thus prove helpful aids in analysing discourse and texts (Mooney, 2004: 899) but are not without limitations. Most of the criticisms articulated against Grice seem to fall into three broad categories: criticisms towards his views on meaning and communication, criticisms towards the notion of conversational maxims, and, finally, criticisms towards the treatment of implicature. There is a degree of overlapping among these categories.

To begin with, cooperation and goal-orientation, presented as principal features of communication, have attracted a series of critical comments. It has been claimed that the premise upon which the CP is based, namely that the purpose or direction of a communicative event can be identified at all times, is erroneous (Kasher, 1998: 185). More specifically, it is observed that the cooperation requirement is often not fulfilled in communication (Davis, 1998). In addition, Green (1990) argues that communicative goals are mutually modelled and perpetually construed rather than simply shared as Grice maintains (cited in Marmaridou, 2000: 238). Goals, like all contextual

40  *Navigating interpersonal meaning and communicative styles*

elements, can "both shape and be shaped by the ongoing interaction" (Baker, 2006: 325).

The critique of the conversational maxims revolves largely around their alleged universality and rationality. Keenan (1998) is not at all comfortable with the ease with which Grice takes for granted that people behave in the ways stipulated by the maxims and provides empirical data of conversational practices in Madagascar; her major finding is that Malagasy speakers tend to be deliberately as uninformative as possible, thus not observing the maxim of Quantity on a regular basis. Still, she recognises that the Gricean framework can serve as a basis for comparing the conversational principles of different speech communities (ibid). Gazdar agrees that the "Gricean maxims are only reasonable and rational relative to a given culture, community, state of affairs" (1979: 54–55). We should also bear in mind that the Gricean maxims of Quality and Manner can be overridden by other conversational factors like politeness and tolerance towards taboo language which are cross-culturally variable (Baker, 2011: 245). On the basis of all the above, and given that Grice's focus is exclusively on monolingual communication in English and on concepts that tend to be cherished in the English-speaking world, such as brevity and sincerity, his approach has unsurprisingly been characterised as "ethnocentric" (ibid: 198). Grice has also been attacked for prescriptiveness (Chapman, 2005: 191). Both the CP and the four maxims are expressed in the imperative form. Even when he revisits "Logic and Conversation", Grice labels the maxims as "conversational imperatives" resembling "moral commandments" (Grice, 1998: 178). These lexico-syntactic choices seem to give his theory a rather prescriptive hue (Chapman, 2005).

Thomas identifies two more problematic aspects of the conversational maxims (1995: 87–92). Firstly, some of the four maxims differ in nature and order (ibid: 91), a shortcoming recognised by Grice himself (1998: 179). For example, the maxim of Quality is fairly easy to grasp; its observance is a matter of yes or no (Thomas, 1995: 91). Adhering to Quantity and Manner, though, is not so straightforward and appears to be more a matter of degree (ibid). Secondly, as Thomas correctly observes, there is always the possibility of maxims overlapping, namely two maxims being invoked at the same time (ibid: 91–92). In general, the multiplicity of maxims has been frequently considered a weakness, since it can result in clashes (Sperber & Wilson, 1995: 389; Davis, 1998: 98). Interestingly enough, as Thomas points out, "the maxim of Relation seems to be always in operation – unless you assume that a contribution is in some way relevant to what has gone before, you will not begin to look for an implicature" (ibid: 92). Yet, Relation is rather neglected within the Gricean framework and requires further elaboration, a need acknowledged by Grice himself (1975/1991: 308). Sperber and Wilson have undertaken this task in proposing a fully-fledged Relevance Theory (Sperber & Wilson, 1986, 1995) which is presented in section 3.2.3.

The role of inference in Gricean framework appears rather questionable, as well. In the first place, it is highly doubtful whether in recovering speaker meaning, interlocutors actually engage in the extensive, conscious discursive

*Implicature* 41

reasoning suggested by Grice's working out schema (Sperber & Wilson, 2002: 9). The terms *implicature* and *inference* are potential sources of misunderstanding, since Grice never really clarifies their difference. Davis (1998) warns against the assimilation of speaker meaning to communication and of implicature to inference, stressing that what a speaker means or implies is determined by his/her intentions, but the latter are independent of the hearer's beliefs or inferences. Thomas shares Davis's concern with the distinction between implicature and inference, drawing attention to the fact that the two terms are often erroneously used interchangeably (1995: 58). She explains their difference as follows:

> To imply is to hint, suggest or convey some meaning indirectly *by means of language* . . . An implicature is generated intentionally by the speaker and *may (or may not)* be understood by the hearer. To infer is to deduce something from something from evidence (this evidence may be *linguistic, paralinguistic, or non-linguistic*). An inference is produced by the hearer.
> (Thomas, 1995: 58; emphasis added)

The rather superficial way in which Grice treats the indeterminacy of PCIs is an additional indication of the occasional vagueness and informality his theory suffers from. Cooren and Sanders argue that if implicatures were as open-ended as Grice suggests, indirect communication would not be feasible (2002: 1046). Somehow, a single interpretation is selected as the most plausible, but when it comes to the specification of the criteria for this selection Grice is reticent (ibid).

Grice's account of tropes, i.e., metaphor, irony, overstatement, and understatement, has not escaped criticism either. Sperber and Wilson raise substantial objections to the attribution of loose talk to floutings of the maxim of Quality (1991: 540–542; cf. Carston, 2002: 115). Figurative language is too prevalent in everyday discourse to be viewed as a mere departure from a norm of literalness or truthfulness (Sperber & Wilson, 1991: 541; cf. Lakoff & Johnson, 1981). Gibbs, based on experimental evidence, claims that the processing of literal meaning neither necessarily precedes nor is a prerequisite for the processing of irony and sarcasm (1986: 4). As opposed to the Gricean account, it is observed that ironic meaning can be recovered directly (ibid; Gibbs & O'Brien, 1991).

On the whole, it could be deduced that implicature and indirectness, in general, are not as straightforward as Grice would like them to be. Much more is involved in indirect communication than sole maxim non-observance (Brumark, 2005). Since there are different kinds of indirectness, fulfilling different functions in different contexts, the Gricean approach to indirectness and implicature presents the analyst with certain difficulties when applied to empirical data (ibid). In particular, it has been found that it cannot efficiently cater for features of communication between intimates, such as verbal humour (ibid; cf. Mooney, 2004: 915). As far as Grice's typology of implicature *per se* is concerned, it has been argued, and justifiably so, that the distinction

42   *Navigating interpersonal meaning and communicative styles*

between what is said and what is implicated is far too rigid (Carston, 2002b: 109) and is rendered even more problematic by the concept of conventional implicature (Levinson, 2000: 15). By the same token, Sperber and Wilson (1995) argue that there are degrees of explicitness and implicitness.

Needless to say, the aforementioned shortcomings by no means undermine the value of Grice's approach. Grice explored new, intriguing areas of verbal communication like implicature, breathing new life into linguistics and continues to inspire pragmatic research. As Fauconnier (1986) puts it, in an era when linguists focused almost exclusively on morphology and syntax, "Grice . . . opened Pandora's box" (cited in Chapman, 2005).

### 3.2.3   Relevance theory and implicature

Embarking on a substantially more cognitive approach to human communication, Relevance Theory (henceforth RT), seeks to address some of the problematic aspects of the Gricean programme (Wilson, 1994: 55–57). Their theory has evolved gradually; it was first introduced by Sperber and Wilson in *Relevance: Communication and Cognition* (1986) followed by updated versions by the same authors in 1987a, 1995, 2002, and 2004. Here, the main aspects of RT will be discussed, with particular emphasis on the way implicature is catered for in this framework.

#### A cognitive psychological theory

Interlocutors are largely unaware of the remarkable array of cognitive processes taking place with lightning speed in the course of communication (Fauconnier, 2004: 658). Cognitive scientists, like cognitive psychologists, cognitive linguists, and psycholinguists, study *inter alia* the system underpinning our ability to communicate and, in particular, to produce and understand language. Clearly situating pragmatics within the realm of cognitive science, Sperber and Wilson set out to investigate verbal communication from a primarily psychological perspective, as opposed to the philosophical approaches prevalent in the twentieth century (Carston et al., 2002).

The core principle RT is that "every aspect of communication and cognition is governed by the search for relevance" (Wilson, 1994: 46). As interactants we tend to pay attention to information which we expect to be relevant to us at a given moment (ibid). Relevance comes in varying degrees; we select a specific input not merely because it is relevant but, crucially, because it is the most relevant input available to us in a particular environment (Wilson & Sperber, 2004: 609). Put differently, a piece of information is worth attending to when it achieves *positive cognitive effect*s (ibid).

As Sperber and Wilson explain, *cognitive effects* are the contextual effects in the cognitive system of an individual, namely changes in his/her beliefs (Sperber & Wilson, 1995: 265). Section 1.2.2 demonstrated the importance of sociophysical context in utterance interpretation, but we should bear in mind that

*Implicature* 43

context in RT is first and foremost "a psychological construct, a subset of . . . [one's] assumptions about the world" (Sperber & Wilson, 1995: 15). A cognitive effect is the result of the interplay between new information and already existing assumptions (Wilson & Sperber, 2004: 608; cf. Sperber & Wilson, 1995: 45). Specifically, humans are interested in obtaining *positive cognitive effects* (Wilson & Sperber, 2004: 608). A *positive cognitive effect* (e.g., a true conclusion) is described as a cognitive effect that promotes the achievement of cognitive goals or the completion of cognitive functions (ibid; Sperber & Wilson, 1995: 265). The interaction between old and new information may cause three kinds of cognitive effect: *contextual strengthening, contradiction,* and *contextual implication* (ibid). Namely, a new input conveyed by the speaker can strengthen an existing assumption of the addressee, contradict and eliminate it, or combine with it to produce a contextual implication (ibid). Contextual implication is the most significant type of cognitive effect; it is a deduction that can be reached neither from input nor context alone but from a combination of the two (ibid).

However, the presence of cognitive effects is not sufficient in itself to guarantee relevance (Wilson & Sperber, 2004: 608). Cognitive effects are yielded by mental processes, which by default require an amount of effort (Sperber & Wilson, 1995: 24). In contrast to cognitive effects, processing effort negatively affects the degree of relevance (ibid). Hence, relevance is defined in terms of cognitive effects and processing effort.

### Relevance of an input to an individual

a. Other things being equal, the greater the positive cognitive effects achieved by processing an input, the greater the relevance of the input to the individual at that time.
b. Other things being equal, the greater the processing effort expended, the lower the relevance of the input to the individual at that time.

(Wilson & Sperber, 2004: 609)

Example 1 that follows illustrates how the degrees of relevance of various inputs can be compared (Desilla, 2009):

---

**Example 1**

*Vivien is pregnant and is planning to spend the weekend with her husband, Paul, at a friend's house. She dislikes pets and particularly avoids cats for fear of toxoplasmosis, a disease that can be transmitted to humans from cats and may cause miscarriage. Vivien asks Paul whether their friends have any pets. Paul could provide any of the three following answers:*

a) Yes, they have two pets.
b) Yes, they have a cat.
c) Yes, they have a fluffy tomcat called Thomas.

---

## 44  *Navigating interpersonal meaning and communicative styles*

Given the definition of relevance, all three answers would be relevant to Vivien, but (b) would be more relevant than both (a) and (c). Firstly, the utterance "Yes, they have a cat" would be more relevant than (a) because it yields more cognitive effects: (a) is an entailment of (b) and, therefore, the latter yields all the conclusions deducible from the former as well as additional conclusions. Secondly, (b) would be more relevant than (c) due to the amount of processing effort involved: despite the fact that both utterances yield the same cognitive effect, (c) requires more processing effort since it contains more linguistic information than (b), information which would seem superfluous in this context. Thus, when similar amounts of effort are required the effect factor is crucial, whereas when similar effects can be yielded the effort factor makes the difference (Wilson & Sperber, 2004: 610). On the basis of the above, it can be argued that an utterance is optimally relevant if (a) it yields adequate contextual effects to deserve the addressee's attention *and* (b) it requires the addressee to expend no unnecessary effort in recovering those effects (Wilson, 1994: 47).

Sperber and Wilson argue that human cognitive efficiency ultimately resides in the ability to select from the environment and memory information which is worth combining, i.e., which yields maximum cognitive effects with minimum processing effort (2002: 14). As the authors maintain, in the evolution of human kind there has been a constant demand for greater cognitive efficiency (ibid; cf. Wilson & Sperber, 2004: 610). This universal tendency is encapsulated in the *First or Cognitive Principle of Relevance*.

### Cognitive Principle of Relevance

Human cognition tends to be geared to the maximisation of relevance.

(Wilson & Sperber, 2004: 610)

The Cognitive Principle of Relevance establishes the cognitive setting in which *ostensive inferential communication*, the model proposed by Sperber and Wilson for human communication, occurs (Wilson & Sperber, 2004: 610). Grice was one of the first to acknowledge the importance of inference in linguistic communication, and his pioneering work paved the way for the emergence of the inferential model. Nonetheless, the pivotal role of inference is not securely established in the Gricean theory of meaning and conversation, since it is limited to the derivation of conversational implicatures (Sperber & Wilson, 2002: 6–9). Inference seems to be absent from the recovery of explicit meaning, which thus must be almost exclusively carried out via decoding processes (ibid: 9). By contrast, Sperber and Wilson firmly believe, as I will attempt to demonstrate shortly, that inference operates in the derivation of implicit as well as explicit meaning (ibid: 9).

What is more, Sperber and Wilson have revamped the notion of context. In RT, context does not solely consist of the immediate socio-physical context and co-text of an utterance; it is rather conceptualised as potentially including a whole range of assumptions that addressee(s) entertain about the world, such as encyclopaedic and cultural knowledge, memories, assumptions about the communicator, etc. (Sperber & Wilson, 1995: 16–17). Contrary to Grice and other pragmatic theories in which context is static and *a priori* determined, in RT context is organically shaped during interaction (Sperber & Wilson, 1998: 374). An RT tool that can help us understand how context is selected is the coinage *cognitive environment* (Sperber & Wilson, 1995: 30). A cognitive environment encompasses all the assumptions or facts that we may perceive or infer, including anything available to interactants through senses, memory, culture, and communication (ibid; Hill, 2006).

As Hill (2006: 14) points out, "[an] utterance does not evoke the audience's entire cognitive environment. It only evokes certain assumptions, and these form the context in which the utterance is processed". Speakers do not just grope in their cognitive environment for the intended context; they specifically search in the area of their cognitive environment they assume they share with the speaker, since the latter cannot possibly intend to communicate assumptions that s/he is unaware of (ibid: 27). It should be stressed that mutual cognitive environment is what the communicator and the addressee(s) *assume* is shared and not necessarily what is *actually* shared (ibid). Thus, the communication parties may share certain assumptions without knowing it and conversely; they may think they share certain assumptions whereas in reality they do not (ibid; Sperber & Wilson, 1995: 35–46). In the second case the risk of communication failure is particularly high because the audience may select an unintended context or may be unable to find any context whatsoever in which to process the utterance (Hill, 2006: 19).

Having thus redefined the concept of context and introduced that of cognitive environment, Sperber and Wilson present their own model of inferential communication, cherishing two central ideas of the Gricean heritage, namely that (a) communication entails the expression and recognition of intentions and (b) utterances automatically raise expectations that lead the addressee towards speaker meaning.

As mentioned previously, the cognitive environment of an individual is in essence a collection of assumptions available to him/her. But what kind of assumptions does an individual tend to entertain? In other words, what kind of information is worth retrieving and processing? The answer is provided by the Cognitive Principle of Relevance (Sperber & Wilson, 1995: 46). Humans have the tendency to turn their attention to information which is maximally relevant (ibid: 49). Given this, a communicator may produce a stimulus which will presumably capture the addressee's attention, trigger certain contextual assumptions, and guide him/her towards an intended conclusion (Wilson & Sperber, 2004: 611). In line with Grice, Sperber and Wilson point out that inferential communication or, more precisely, *ostensive inferential communication*, involves two layers of intention.

## 46 *Navigating interpersonal meaning and communicative styles*

### Ostensive-inferential communication

a. The informative intention: the intention to inform the audience of something.
b. The communicative intention: the intention to inform the audience of one's informative intention.

(Wilson & Sperber, 2004: 611)

The recognition of the informative intention on behalf of the addressee is a pre-requisite for comprehension (Wilson & Sperber, 2004: 611). Ostensive stimuli can be verbal, non-verbal, or multimodal, and aim at drawing the addressee's attention to the meaning conveyed by the communicator (ibid). Internet memes, such as the Baby Yoda memes included in the warm-up exercise, are excellent cases in point. As Scott (2022: 120) highlights, regardless of whether you are posting your own meme creation or somebody else's, "sharing is an ostensive act of communication" and is precisely what endows the meme with its "fundamentally communicative nature". Meme creators have an array of stylistic resources in their arsenal (e.g., irony, self-deprecating humour, intertextuality) which may demand surplus cognitive effort but surely lead to rewarding cognitive effects; think of that feeling of gratification when you decipher a wordplay, the "intertextual pleasure" (Zappavigna, 2012: 101) when you recognise an indirect cultural reference, or, perhaps, that sense of shared experience and social bonding when you are able to identify with the situation portrayed in a meme (Scott, 2022).

Thus, an ostensive stimulus creates clear expectations of relevance: the addressee of an ostensive stimulus is encouraged (by the communicator) to formulate the presumption that it is adequately relevant to deserve his/her attention and processing (ibid: 611–612). This brings us to the *Second or Communicative Principle of Relevance*.

### Communicative Principle of Relevance

Every ostensive stimulus conveys a presumption of its own optimal relevance.

(Wilson & Sperber, 2004: 612)

In turn, *optimal relevance* specifies the audience's expectations in terms of effort and effect.

### Presumption of Optimal Relevance

a. The ostensive stimulus is relevant enough to be worth the audience's processing effort.
b. It is the most relevant one compatible with communicator's *abilities* and *preferences*.

(Wilson & Sperber, 2004: 612; emphasis added)

*Implicature* 47

Premise (b) is particularly significant, since it pertains to what the communicator is willing and able to produce (Wilson & Sperber, 2004: 613; cf. Sperber & Wilson, 1995: 266–278). On the one hand, the communicator's ultimate aim is to ensure understanding (Wilson & Sperber, 2004: 612). To this end, s/he needs to convey the ostensive stimulus in such a way as to make it readily comprehensible, as well as to offer some indication of the cognitive effects s/he intends to achieve (ibid: 612). In addition, Sperber and Wilson underscore that it is the communicator's responsibility to make the correct assumptions about the audience's cognitive environment; the communicator is the one who determines how difficult (or how easy) the comprehension process will be (1995: 43). On the other hand, communicators can be expected neither to know everything nor to act against their interests and predilections (Wilson & Sperber, 2004: 613). Often, there can be relevant stimuli that the communicator is unwilling or unable to produce, or ever think of, at a given moment (ibid).

*The comprehension procedure: explicatures and implicatures*

In RT, understanding utterances involves two distinct types of cognitive process, namely decoding and inference. However, as opposed to Grice who restricts the role of inferential processes to the calculation of implicatures, Sperber and Wilson show that pragmatic inference is also employed in determining explicit meaning, since linguistically encoded information is hardly ever a fully-fledged proposition (1995: 182; Carston, 1998). As becomes obvious in the following, the inferential phase of comprehension, which takes the addressee from decoded linguistic meaning to a hypothesis about speaker meaning, is controlled by the Communicative Principle of Relevance as well as the Presumption of Optimal Relevance (Wilson & Sperber, 2004: 613; cf. Carston, 1998).

**Relevance-theoretic comprehension procedure**

a. Follow a path of least effort in computing cognitive effects: test interpretive hypotheses (disambiguations, reference resolutions, implicatures, etc.) in order of accessibility.
b. Stop when your expectations of relevance are satisfied (or abandoned).

There are two points worth noting here: firstly, the hearer expects the speaker to make (in accordance with his/her abilities and predilections) his/her utterances as easily comprehensible as possible (Wilson & Sperber, 2004: 613–614). Based on that premise, the addressee follows the path of the least effort (ibid). Secondly, the cause for clause (b) resides in that there should always be only a single relevant interpretation (ibid). If a speaker wishes his/her utterance to be readily understood, s/he should try to produce it in such a way in order to ensure that the first interpretation to satisfy the addressee's

## 48 *Navigating interpersonal meaning and communicative styles*

expectations of relevance is the actually intended interpretation (ibid: 614). The addressee carries out a number of tasks in the pursuit of communicated meaning.

**Subtasks in the overall comprehension process**

a. Constructing an appropriate hypothesis about explicit content (explicatures) via decoding, disambiguation, reference resolution, and other pragmatic enrichment processes.
b. Constructing an appropriate hypothesis about the intended contextual assumptions (implicated premises).
c. Constructing an appropriate hypothesis about the intended contextual implications (implicated conclusions).

(Adapted from Wilson & Sperber, 2004: 615)

We should bear in mind that the enumeration used here for the purposes of presentation by no means implies that the sub-tasks take place in sequential order (Wilson & Sperber, 2004: 615). As Sperber and Wilson stress, "hypotheses about explicatures, implicated premises and implicated conclusions are developed in parallel against a background of expectations which may be revised or elaborated as the utterance unfolds" (ibid). Before exemplifying how the overall comprehension mechanism works, it is necessary to explain certain concepts and tasks, starting with the term *explicature*.

The explicature of an utterance is an explicitly communicated assumption recovered by the identification of *propositional form* or simply *proposition* (Sperber & Wilson, 1995: 182–183). Eliciting the propositional form of an utterance involves more often than not *enrichment*. Enrichment is the process whereby the content conveyed by an utterance comes to incorporate elements that are contextually implied without being part of the locution; reference assignment and disambiguation are the main tasks that the addressee carries out to this end (Cummings, 2023: 54). Thus, explicature is not exhausted in truth-conditional content but is much richer (ibid). Most importantly, RT allows for degrees of explicitness; for Sperber and Wilson, "an explicature is a combination of linguistically encoded and contextually inferred features. The smaller the relative contribution of the contextual features, the more explicit the explicature and inversely" (1995: 182).

Within the RT framework, *implicatures* are defined as contextual assumptions or implications arising from the communicator's intention and the addressee's expectation that the utterance of the former is optimally relevant (Sperber & Wilson, 1995: 194–195). A distinction is drawn between *implicated premises* and *implicated conclusions*: implicated premises are mainly accessible from the addressee's background knowledge and memory whereas implicated conclusions can be deduced from the context and the explicatures of an utterance processed together (ibid: 195). Any intended implicated premises and implicated conclusions are included in the first

*Implicature* 49

interpretation of an utterance that complies with the principle of relevance (ibid). Understandably, the implicated conclusions derived from processing an utterance can, in turn, be used as relevant implicated premises in processing the next utterance and so on (ibid: 118). What should also be stressed in the relevance-theoretic account of implicature is that indirectness in an utterance augments contextual effects, while simultaneously increasing processing effort (ibid: 235). Therefore, in the pursuit of optimal relevance, speakers need to achieve the appropriate equilibrium between these two variables (cf. Blakemore, 1992: 34).

Because explicitness is seen as a matter of degree, at first glance, it would seem that the boundaries between the explicature and implicature(s) of an utterance become fuzzier in the relevance-theoretic framework. Yet, there are valid counterarguments. Carston affirms that the implicature(s) of an utterance can be distinguished from its explicature by employing the criterion of *functional independence* (1988: 156–157). She proceeds, stating that "implicatures have distinct propositional forms with their own truth-conditions and . . . function independently of the explicature" (ibid: 157). In other words, an utterance does not entail implicatures, it *evokes* implicatures (Hill, 2006: 19). What is more, an explicature only expresses information that is already known, whereas implicated conclusions are in essence new information (ibid).

With respect to implicature (in)determinacy, Sperber and Wilson seem to adopt a stance akin to Grice's, rejecting the view that implicatures are always fully determinate assumptions (1995: 195–200). Instead, they suggest that the implicatures of an utterance can have varying degrees of strength (ibid: 199). Thus, an implicature may be *strong*, i.e., highly predictable, or *weak*, i.e., not easily determinable. The more restricted the range of possible premises or conclusions among which the hearer can choose, the stronger the implicatures (ibid).

Having explained certain key concepts, let us now illustrate the various sub-tasks of the overall comprehension procedure by means of the exchange between Jack and Alice that was analysed from the Gricean perspective in 3.2.2 (adapted from Desilla, 2019b: 252).[6] We are interested in the comprehension of Alice's utterance by Jack and, in particular, its implicatures.

Taking for granted that Alice would like to spend the night with him, what Jack wants to know is whether she prefers them to spend the night at his or her place, and, thus, he assumes in (b) that Alice's utterance will achieve relevance by replying to his question. As evident, Alice has not provided a direct answer to Jack's question and, therefore, Jack needs to infer an implicated answer. On this basis, the possibility of Alice referring to $GALAXY_2$ is eliminated. One of the encoded logical forms provides easy access to the assumption in (d) and then to the assumption in (e). These can function as the two implicated premises which together with the explicature in (f), identified via the enrichment of the logical form, can yield the implicated conclusion in (g). In turn, the strongly implicated conclusion processed together with

50  *Navigating interpersonal meaning and communicative styles*

*Table 3.2.3* Subtasks of the comprehension procedure

| | |
|---|---|
| a) Alice has said to Jack, "$I_x$d rather eat a GALAXY$_1$/ GALAXY$_2$." [$I_x$ = easily interpretable pronoun: speaker is referent] [GALAXY$_1$ = chocolate] [GALAXY$_2$ = a very large group of stars held together in the universe] | Embedding of the decoded (incomplete) logical form of Alice's utterance into a description of Alice's ostensive behaviour. Reference assignment and disambiguation starts. |
| b) Alice's utterance will be optimally relevant to Jack. | Expectation raised by recognition of Alice's ostensive behaviour and acceptance of the presumption of relevance it conveys. |
| c) Alice's utterance will achieve relevance by providing an answer to Jack's indirect invitation to spend the night together. | Expectation raised by (b), together with the facts that such an answer would be most relevant to Jack at this point. |
| d) GALAXY$_1$ is a chocolate. | First assumption to occur to Jack, which, together with other appropriate premises, might satisfy expectation (c). Accepted as the first implicated premise of Alice's utterance. |
| e) Chocolate is considered a substitute for sexual pleasure. | Second assumption to occur to Jack, which, together with assumption in (d) and other appropriate premises, might satisfy expectation (c). Accepted as the second implicated premise of Alice's utterance. |
| f) Alice would rather eat a chocolate, than spend the night with Jack. | First enrichment of the logical form of Alice's utterance to occur to Jack, which might combine with (d) and (e) to lead to the satisfaction of (c). Accepted as an explicature of Alice's utterance. |
| g) Alice refuses to spend the night with Jack because she prefers a substitute for sexual pleasure, instead. | Inferred from (d), (e), and (f) satisfying (c). Accepted as a strong implicated conclusion of Alice's utterance. |
| h) <br> – Alice is not at all attracted to Jack. <br> – Alice is irritated by Jack's coarse flirting. <br> – Alice likes Jack but thinks it is too early to spend the night with him. | Inferred from (g) plus background knowledge. Three of an array of possible weak implicatures of Alice's utterance, which together with (g) satisfy expectation (b). |

background knowledge might generate a series of weak implicatures, like those included in (h). The extra cognitive effort called for by Alice's indirect response is counterbalanced by extra cognitive effects, namely the strongly communicated implicature in (g) and possibly other weakly communicated implicatures exemplified in (h). The tones of mockery conveyed by Alice's utterance can be added to the surplus effects (cf. Desilla, 2019b: 252).

The comprehension procedure from earlier shows that explicatures and implicatures (implicated premises and conclusions alike) are recovered via

*Implicature* 51

what Wilson and Sperber describe as "a process of mutual parallel adjustment", whereby hypotheses about both are made rapidly, on-line and in order of accessibility (2004, 617; Carston, 2002: 137). Thus, the hearer expands the context (e.g., by adding background knowledge to the immediately accessible contextual assumptions) until an interpretation that would satisfy his/her expectation of relevance emerges (Sperber & Wilson, 1998: 378–382).

*Style being the relationship*

The style of communication reflects the speaker's assumptions about the addressee's cognitive abilities, his/her level of attention, how much the speaker intends to facilitate the processing of his/her utterance, as well as the degree of perceived, claimed, or actual intimacy between the interlocutors (Sperber & Wilson, 1995: 217). In fact, it seems that the larger the number of implicatures included in the speaker's utterances the higher the presumed degree of closeness and mutuality between him/her and the addressee (ibid: 218). As Sperber and Wilson aptly remark, "style is the relationship" (ibid: 217).

Style emerges in the pursuit of relevance and so do the classical figures of speech, such as metaphor and irony (ibid: 219–224). In particular, it is argued that poetic effects arise when accessing a great number of (very) weak implicatures in the course of achieving relevance (ibid: 224). Therefore, as one may well expect, RT treats instances of figurative language neither as deviations from a norm of literalness nor as floutings/exploitations of a maxim of truthfulness, but as stemming from the interpretive use of language (Sperber & Wilson, 1991: 541–542; cf. Wilson & Sperber, 2004: 619).

According to Sperber and Wilson, two types of representation can be found in an utterance: an utterance may describe a certain state of affairs (*descriptive use*) or interpret a certain thought (*interpretive use*) (Wilson & Sperber, 1988: 133). Nonetheless, at the deepest level all utterances are regarded as interpretive representations of the speaker's thoughts (Sperber & Wilson, 1995: 231). This relationship is technically referred to as *interpretive resemblance* (Sperber & Wilson, 1991: 542). In such a framework, metaphor is based on an interpretive relation between the propositional form of the utterance and the thought represented by the latter (ibid).

In the relevance-theoretic account of metaphor, the hearer never tests the literal interpretation first; only when a loose interpretation thwarts his/her expectation of relevance would s/he start to consider a more literal interpretation (Wilson & Sperber, 2004: 609). Let us revisit Darla's utterance "I'm a piranha". The propositional form of this utterance interpretively resembles what she wishes to communicate to her uncle, the dentist, namely the assumptions that she has very sharp teeth, can/will bite others, and so on (Desilla, 2005: 24) These are actually the implicated conclusions of Darla's utterance, which are recovered via the joint processing of a set of implicated premises (piranhas have razor sharp teeth, a strong bite, and so on) as well as immediate contextual premises available through the visuals and soundtrack.

## 52 *Navigating interpersonal meaning and communicative styles*

Needless to say, the more creative the metaphor, the weaker the implicatures generated, and the greater the hearer's effort in recovering them (Sperber & Wilson, 1995: 235–236).

Interestingly enough, the concept of interpretive resemblance has also had quite an appeal within translation studies. More specifically, according to Gutt (1998: 200), an original text and its translation interpretively resemble one another. In other words, a translator restates in the target language (TL) what the creator of the source-text (ST) said or wrote in the source-language (SL). Since interpretive resemblance has varying degrees, the number of shared explicatures and implicatures depends on how faithful or free the target version is (Gutt, 1998). Furthermore, the translator, who assumes the role of the communicator, is the one responsible for helping the target audience in the search for optimal relevance; as Díaz-Pérez (2013: 292) explains, the translator essentially undertakes the balancing act of catering for two distinct cognitive environments by adopting "the most suitable strategy to reproduce the cognitive effects intended by the ST communicator with the lowest possible effort on the part of the target receptor".

Because of its cognitive-psychological foundations, RT has been recommended as one of the best theories to account for the comprehension of humorous discourse (Yus, 2003, 2016, 2021; Solska, 2012; Scott, 2022). In an attempt to show how relevance-theoretical insights can be applied to the analysis of wordplays which pose significant challenges to translators (cf. Delabastita, 1994; Asimakoulas, 2004), let us revisit one of the memes of the warm-up exercise along with its Italian version (Baby Yoda Italia, online).

---

**Example 2**

EN: When you click "accept cookies" and then you don't get any cookies.
IT: Quando clichi "accept cookies" ma poi nessuno ti porta i biscotti.
BT: When you click "accept cookies" but then nobody brings you the biscuits.

---

The meme token in question belongs to the Baby Yoda meme family. Baby Yoda, also known as "Grogu" or "the Child", is one of the characters of *The Mandalorian* first aired on Disney+ in 2019 and has become a meme sensation ever since with several dedicated accounts across social media and languages. The Baby Yoda meme family almost exclusively consists of multimodal memes, featuring one or more images of Baby Yoda himself with one or more text captions. Playfulness and humour emerge precisely from the co-deployment and interplay of the verbal and visual aspects (Yus, 2018). What is more, whenever wordplay is part of this *multimodal ensemble* (Jewitt, 2013) the meme is intended to trigger the enrichment tasks of disambiguation and reference resolution (Zenner & Geeraerts, 2018; Scott,

2022). Hence, the meme creator can envisage, and to an extent, control, the inferential process and the accessibility of explicatures and implicatures on the addressee's part.

The present meme features the image of a rather disappointed and miserable-looking Baby Yoda wrapped up in his brown robe and a caption involving a pun based on the polysemy of the lexical item *cookie*: the two pun-related meanings expressed are ($COOKIE_1$), i.e., "a piece of information stored on your computer about internet documents that you have looked at" and ($COOKIE_2$), i.e., "a small, flat, sweet food made from flour and sugar" (https://dictionary.cambridge.org/dictionary/english/cookie). Following Yus's (2021) classification regarding punning structure, it seems that here we are dealing with the *one meaning then another* scenario; the two meanings are not entertained in parallel but rather ($COOKIE_1$) is activated first followed by ($COOKIE_2$) at a later stage. As Scott (2022) observes, memes work as *multimodal metaphors* encouraging addressees to access an array of pertinent weak implicatures, accompanied by tones of gentle self-mockery.

Although the present meme could make perfect sense on its own and be interpreted by accessing a weak implicated conclusion along the lines of, e.g., *without cookies I feel miserable/frustrated*, it is designed to activate an additional range of implicated premises by virtue of belonging to the Baby Yoda meme family where he is often portrayed craving or relishing coffee, pizza, chicken nuggets, and his favourite cookies. In particular, Baby Yoda has been established as a cookie lover since Episode 4, Season 2 of *The Mandalorian* when he devoured a whole box of blue cookies resembling French macarons. His addiction to these blue cookies is the theme of several memes, as evidenced in the warm-up exercise of this chapter.

As manifestations *par excellence* of participatory culture (Marwick, 2013), memes have been prime material for remediation and translation alike. In the Italian version, the creator has preserved the collocation "accept cookies" intact as a *loan* or *borrowing* (Vinay & Darbelnet, 1958/1977), instead of the software localisation option "accettare i cookies", while rendering the second occurrence of cookies as "biscotti". This strategy is fairly similar to what Díaz-Pérez (2014: 118–119) calls "sacrifice of the pun and maintenance of (part of semantic content) whereby the translator prioritises the meaning layer that s/he considers more relevant; by spelling out the meaning of the sweet crunchy snack in the end; however, the translator inevitably tampers with the degree of implicitness/explicitness as envisaged by the creator of the original meme, thus potentially lowering the number of positive cognitive effects as well as the degree of interpretive resemblance between the two versions. The very juxtaposition of "cookies" and "biscotti" which can be treated as *co-hyponyms* belonging to the same *semantic field* (cf. Baker, 2011) ensures that the style is still playful and the joke remains language-dependent to an extent, albeit requiring an ever so slightly different comprehension procedure path; both source-text (ST) and target-text (TT) rely on the audience's

## 54 Navigating interpersonal meaning and communicative styles

IT knowledge but the ambiguity is presumably more readily resolved in the Italian text because of the lexical item "biscotti".

### Mini discussion of RT

Sperber and Wilson's theory has had substantial implications and innumerable applications in various scientific domains. As far as pragmatics is concerned, RT undoubtedly brought a fresh breeze into the field. By proposing a "cognitively plausible pragmatic theory", Sperber and Wilson initiated the transition from philosophical pragmatics to cognitive pragmatics (Carston et al., 2002; Recanati, 1987: 729). Crucial pragmatic concepts are re-defined and analysed from a novel perspective. First of all, inference is given due attention and elaborated, and its pivotal role in communication is established (cf. Levinson, 1989). Moreover, Sperber and Wilson offer an original view of context which clearly reflects the dynamic nature of communicative events (cf. Yus Ramos, 1998; Baker, 2006: 324–327). In their framework, context ceases to be static and predetermined, and acquires plasticity; it is constructed by the interlocutors in the actual conversation and can be repeatedly expanded in the comprehension process until an appropriate interpretation is reached. As Yus Ramos observes, the bi-directional influence of context is revealed; namely, context is determined by conversants but simultaneously delimits the interpretation of utterances (1998: 309; cf. Wilson, 1994).

Perhaps the most important legacy of RT resides in the account of comprehension in general, and implicature in particular. The comprehension process is accounted for in a holistic way, since both explicit and implicit content are derived in terms of the same principle, i.e., relevance. Moreover, we are offered a distinction between explicature and implicature which is much more transparent than that put forward by Grice (cf. Carston, 1998: 22). The aforementioned uniformity of Sperber and Wilson's approach is evident in the treatment of implicature *per se*; all implicatures, no matter how weak or strong, are recovered via the same inferential processes (cf. Blakemore, 1987: 130). Overall, there is a momentous shift of focus from the philosophical importance of implicature to the cognitive mechanisms involved in its comprehension, a shift, of course, in keeping with the general psychological foundations of RT.

One of the immediate criticisms that Sperber and Wilson received is that of "overconfidence" (Mey, 1993; cf. Levinson, 1989). According to Mey, accounting for all the phenomena that had been previously treated by a set of maxims with a single principle is a rather extravagant enterprise (1993: 91). In fact, relevance *per se* as a notion has caused some discomfort among a number of scholars. For instance, Bach and Harnish wonder how interlocutors follow the principle of relevance and how processing effort, one of the defining conditions of relevance, can be measured empirically (1987: 711). In addressing the first question, the proponents of RT underscore that there is no such thing as adhering to or violating the principle of relevance, simply

*Implicature* 55

because relevance is neither a maxim nor a rule, but an intrinsic feature of human cognition (Sperber & Wilson, 1987b: 745; Wilson, 1994: 56). As Sperber and Wilson remark, "communicators and audience need no more know the principle of relevance to communicate than they need to know the principles of genetics in order to reproduce" (1987b: 746). With respect to the second issue raised by Bach and Harnish, pertaining to processing effort, Sperber and Wilson draw a distinction between comparative and quantitative concepts, arguing that relevance falls on the comparative side (1987b: 742; cf. Wilson & Sperber, 2004). RT does not offer a measure of processing effort or cognitive effect based on the premise that spontaneous mental workings are difficult to measure (Wilson & Sperber, 2004: 627). However, RT provides the possibility of comparing the actual or expected relevance of two inputs, e.g., of two alternative verbal stimuli, thus allowing researchers to manipulate the factors of effect and effort in experiments (Sperber & Wilson, 1987b).

Regarding the thorny issue of communicative intentions, in the RT framework the addressee can neither decode nor deduce the communicator's communicative intention; the best s/he can do is construct an assumption on the basis of the evidence provided by the communicator's ostensive behaviour. For such an assumption there may be confirmation but no proof. As Gutt (2000: 212) points out, the foregoing claim is fairly plausible since in real life "we make inferences about people's intentions on the basis of their behaviour" all the time. What is also interesting to note is that communication can be successful even when the communicator's intentions are not precisely and entirely perceived by the audience. In RT communication is seen "as a matter of enlarging mutual cognitive environments, not of duplicating thoughts" (Sperber & Wilson, 1995: 193).

With regard to implicature, the postulate that there should always be a single relevant interpretation may seem partly implausible. We should bear in mind that a single instance of implicature is likely to elicit more than one relevant interpretation in a single context. Besides, Sperber and Wilson themselves acknowledge this possibility in proposing the distinction between strong and weak implicatures. Thus, it would be more realistic to argue that the aforementioned postulate is applicable to the interpretation of strong implicatures, due to their high predictability. By contrast, an utterance may generate an array of weak implicatures all satisfying the expectation of optimal relevance.

The applicability of RT to literature, and fictional discourse in general, was another subject of discussion in the early days of the theory. Clark (1987) stated that RT cannot account for fiction due to its inability to cater for *layering*. Fiction involves two layers of communication: between the fictional characters on the one hand, and between the author and his/her readership on the other (ibid). According to Clark (1987), the second layer of communication does not involve communicative or informative intentions and, thus, cannot be explained by the relevance-theoretic framework (ibid: 716).

## 56 Navigating interpersonal meaning and communicative styles

Sperber and Wilson (1987b: 751) tackled this criticism stressing that while reading a novel, every sentence is interpreted in terms of the principle of relevance. The author indeed communicates with the audience by yielding a series of weak cognitive effects, e.g., by guiding the reader to activate certain assumptions or to abandon others (ibid). Similarly, Reboul repudiates Clark's claims indicating that the interpretation of fictional utterances does not occur in a crucially different way from that of the non-fictional utterances and, therefore, the comprehension procedure of RT is equally applicable to literature (1987: 729). Ever since, there have been numerous successful applications RT to both literature and film. Desilla's (2009, 2012, 2014) study of implicatures in subtitled film is a case in point.

### 3.3 Case study

Desilla's research (2009, 2012, 2014) investigates the construal, cross-cultural relay and comprehension of implicatures by filmmakers, translators, and audiences respectively. She proposes an original definition of implicature in the context of subtitled film, adapting the RT concepts of *cognitive environment, immediate contextual premises, implicated premises*, and implicated *conclusions* accordingly to cater for the semiotic complexity of film communication (Desilla, 2012: 34):

> Implicature in film can be defined as any assumption intended by the filmmakers which is implicitly and non-conventionally communicated in the film dialogue. Audiences can infer the intended implicatures via the selection and the joint processing of the most relevant elements from their cognitive environment. The cognitive environment potentially includes information entertained by the viewers themselves as well as information conveyed (perceived or inferred) by the various semiotic resources deployed in the film being viewed. The former may consist, inter alia, of encyclopaedic and sociocultural knowledge, as well as personal experience. The latter may be retrieved via the components of the mise-en-scene, cinematography, editing and soundtrack. The appropriate selection and exploitation of some of the afore-mentioned elements comprising the cognitive environment actually forms the particular context for the recovery of implicated conclusions (strong and weak). The utterance(s) that trigger the implicature(s) are intended by the filmmakers to evoke a specific context: background knowledge will be triggered in the form of implicated premises while the information readily conveyed via the film's image and sound will be selected as immediate contextual premises.

As part of her case study, Desilla analyses 71 instances of implicature identified in *Bridget Jones's Diary* (2001) and *Bridget Jones: The Edge of Reason* (2004), henceforth referred as *BJ1* and *BJ2* respectively, and their Greek

*Implicature*    57

subtitled versions available on DVD. The overwhelming majority of the implicatures comprising the data set can be classified into two broad categories in terms of the way they are relayed in the subtitles, namely *preservation* and *explicitation* (Desilla, 2009/2019b).

The overall tendency in both Bridget Jones films is clearly towards implicature preservation with only a very small number of ST implicatures are on the whole rendered explicitly in the subtitles of the two films (Desilla, 2009/2019b). In what follows, *implicature preservation* and *implicature explicitation* are explained and illustrated. It should be noted that these terms designate the way in which the implicatures of the film dialogue are relayed in the subtitles and do not necessarily represent strategies/techniques consciously applied by the subtitlers themselves. After all, the subtitling process tends to be internalised and subconscious to a certain extent (cf. Kovačič, 1996: 304). As far as the parameters that influence translation choices are concerned, we can merely speculate or make educated guesses.

*Implicature preservation*

Preservation refers to the intact transference of the SL implicature into the TL, which can be succinctly described as 'implicature into same implicature'; the term *preservation* is used in contrast to *explicitation* to denote that no attempt has been made to spell out the implicature in the subtitles (Desilla, 2009/2019b). Effectively, the implicature expressed in the English dialogue does not become part of the explicature of the Greek subtitles. Put differently, translators retain the implicit way in which meaning is encoded and communicated by the filmmakers. It has been found that implicature preservation has often been achieved through a more or less verbatim translation (Desilla, 2009):

EL (Bridget): Great. I was wearing a carpet.
EN: Τέλεια. Φορούσα ένα χαλί.
BT: Perfect. I was wearing a carpet.

Bridget's voice-over from *BJ1* (Maguire, 2001) illustrates an implicature being preserved through literal translation with the exception of the use of the synonym "perfect". In this scene, Bridget is at her mother's Christmas buffet. In the preceding shots, Pam reprimanded Bridget for her choice of clothes, and Bridget hesitantly agreed to change into "something lovely" that her mother Pam had chosen for her. A few moments later, we see Bridget entering the living room, wearing an ensemble with a large red floral print. Kinesics is indicative of Bridget's lack of comfort (immediate contextual premise). In the voice-over Bridget says, "Great. I was wearing a carpet". This metaphor is faithfully rendered in the TL and presumably triggers off a similar set of relevant implicated premises in the mind of the target viewers (i.e., some carpets have flowery motifs with bright colours, ensembles ornamented in bright and

## 58  Navigating interpersonal meaning and communicative styles

floral designs are often considered old-fashioned and/or kitsch, etc.). These implicatures processed together with relevant immediate contextual premises, including the *Can't Take My Eyes Off You* song playing, lead to an array of weak implicated conclusions pertaining to Bridget's feelings towards the garment and perhaps her mother, as well (e.g., Bridget thinks that this ensemble is old-fashioned/kitsch/embarrassing, resents Pam's attempt to promote her as a traditional housewife, etc.). The tones of self-irony/mockery expressed by Bridget's utterance are equally conveyed by the Greek subtitles.

### Implicature explicitation

Explicitation is the process whereby the subtitler spells out (partly or totally) the implicatures of the original dialogue, which can be succinctly referred to as "implicature into explicature" (Desilla, 2009/2019b). ST and TT may still interpretively resemble one another; their difference crucially resides in the style of communication. In other words, what is only evoked in the English utterance (or part thereof) is explicitly stated in the Greek text. Implicatures have been found to be explicitated in a very limited number of instances in the data set (Desilla, 2009/2019b); half of these instances pertain to implicatures triggered by what are referred to in translation studies as *culture-specific items* (Newmark, 1988; Ramière, 2006) or, more recently, *extralinguistic cultural references* (ECRs) (Pedersen, 2011) which can include overt or covert *real-world cultural references* and *intertextual references* or *allusions* (Ranzato, 2016). Explicitness comes in degrees and (Sperber & Wilson, 1995) the same applies to explicitation, as exemplified here (Desilla, 2009):

ST: (Bridget): I'm enjoying a relationship with two men simultaneously. The one called Ben, the other Jerry.

TT1: Απολαμβάνω μια σχέση με δύο άντρες ταυτόχρονα. Τον Παγωτό και τον Σοκολάτα.

BT1: I'm enjoying a relationship with two men simultaneously. The Ice cream [masculine] and the [masculine] Chocolate.

At this point of the film, Bridget has already separated from her boyfriend. The *mise-en-scène* is of paramount importance because it manifests Bridget's emotional status. She is wrapped in a duvet, holding an ice cream tub and dragging herself through the hallway (immediate contextual premises). Scattered on the floor and around the flat are ice cream tubs, magazines, and clothes (immediate contextual premises), clearly suggesting that Bridget has been neglecting domestic chores. The voice-over epitomises how she feels: "I'm enjoying a relationship with two men simultaneously. The one called Ben, the other Jerry" (Kidron, 2004a). The source-audience (SA) presumably recognises Ben and Jerry as an ice cream brand (implicated premise). As a matter of fact, one may discern that Bridget herself holds a *Ben & Jerry's* ice cream tub (immediate contextual premise). The first strong implicated

*Implicature* 59

conclusion emerging from Bridget's utterance is that she is enjoying a relationship with ice cream. Yet, this is in essence another metaphor which in turn generates an array of weak implicated conclusions, namely that Bridget overindulges in food for comfort, is depressed, etc. As the director Beeban Kidron (2004b) affirms, this scene fragment is intended to communicate "the cultural idea of being emotionally under the duvet" after a separation, which is identifiable for many people. The surplus processing effort that Bridget's complex linguistic indirectness seems to require can be compensated for by the recovery of the implicatures, the resulting humour and, of course, the extra tones of self-sarcasm/mockery. By casting a glance at the TT, it becomes evident that the subtitler has ironed out the covert real-world ECR to Ben & Jerry's ice cream. Presumably in an attempt to recreate the figurative and humorous effect, two personifications are used (i.e., Ice Cream and Chocolate) instead. This choice results in a different explicature which gives access to a partly different set of implicated conclusions. It seems that the ST on the whole involves two layers of indirectness owing to the reference to Ben & Jerry's ice-cream, as opposed to the Greek version which has only one. The strongly implicated conclusion of the ST has been integrated into the explicature of the subtitle. Nevertheless, ST and TT are identical in terms of their weak implicatures. The Greek DVD subtitle evokes an additional implicated premise pertaining to the view of chocolate as a substitute for sexual pleasure. Yet, this new implicature by no means undermines the overall communicative intention of the filmmakers; on the contrary, it reinforces the idea of a single Bridget resorting to comfort food. This target version illustrates a rather sophisticated, practically hybrid, way of implicature relay in which part of the implicit meaning is spelt out, another part is preserved, a new implicated premise is evoked, and, for all that, the substance of Bridget's voice-over is successfully conveyed.

The ECR to Ben & Jerry's ice cream represents a rather intriguing case. Ben & Jerry's is originally an American company, founded in Vermont in the late 1970s, but gradually expanded across the globe (Ben & Jerry's, online). Ben & Jerry's international debut was in the UK in 1994 and many other European countries followed thereafter (ibid). However, Ben & Jerry's ice cream was not marketed in Greece in 2004 and, therefore, the average Greek viewer could not have been safely expected to be familiar with this brand. This seems to be the most plausible reason for the explicitation of the relevant implicated premise evoked by Bridget's original utterance (Desilla, 2009). The subtitler has rendered the ECR by means of the superordinate term "ice cream", indicative of the *generalisation* or *explicitation* strategy (Vinay & Darbelnet, 1958/1977; Díaz-Cintas & Remael, 2021). Although the translation of brand names by the concept they represent usually works well from a denotative perspective, the foreign flavour disappears (Díaz-Cintas & Remael, 2007). In this example, possibly as compensation for this loss, and also for the loss of the proper names Ben and Jerry that the ST wordplay is based on, the word "Chocolate" has been added next to "Ice cream", and, hence two

60    *Navigating interpersonal meaning and communicative styles*

personifications have been created in the subtitles through the use of upper-case initials and the masculine article (Desilla, 2009). This handling is akin to Delabastita's (1996) *ST pun to TT related rhetorical device* strategy.

Given that approximately 18 years have passed since the first release of the DVD version of *Bridget Jones: The Edge of Reason* and that Greece has been a market for Ben & Jerry's ice cream for more than a decade, it would be worth casting a glance at the Greek subtitles now available on Netflix (Kidron, 2004b) and reflect on how they compare to the Greek subtitles from the mid-2000s:

TT2: Απολαμβάνω τη σχέση με δύο άντρες ταυτόχρονα/τον Μπεν και τον Τζέρι.
BT2: I'm enjoying the relationship with two men simultaneously/Ben and Jerry.

Here the subtitler has transferred the proper names "Ben and Jerry" through transliteration in Greek, thus preserving the degree of implicitness intact in the TT; no explicitation whatsoever has taken place. The same strategy can be observed in several other languages like Spanish, Czech, and Chinese. The Italian subtitler, however, has followed a different approach (Kidron, 2004b):

TT3: Frequento due uomini contemporaneamente. Uno si chiama Sam e l'altro Montana.
BT3: I am dating with two men simultaneously. The one called Sam the other Montana.

The Italian subtitles mirror the style of the original by replacing the Ben and Jerry wordplay with a new wordplay based on the traditional Italian gelato brand Sammontana (*Sammontana*, online). The need for text reduction cannot really account for this *ST pun to TT pun* strategy (Delabastita, 1996, cf. Díaz-Pérez, 2013) since the preservation of the original names would have led to a shorter rendering. Arguably, the present translation achieves a high degree of relevance for the Italian audience because it enables them to access the implicated conclusion intended by the filmmakers in an equally playful way but without the greater processing effort that the indirect reference to Ben & Jerry's ice cream would require compared to the more familiar and, in all probability, more readily accessible, Sammontana ice cream. However, such *cultural substitutions* (Baker, 2011) or *transpositions* (Díaz-Cintas & Remael, 2021) are not without shortcomings in subtitling: as Díaz-Cintas and Remael (2021: 213) caution, "they can result in a conflict with the foreign culture presented on screen, thus affecting the diegesis of the production and endangering the credibility of the translation" even more so when there are clearly audible names in the original. In the BJ2 scene under analysis, this substitution of Ben and Jerry's with Sammontana ice cream may also jeopardise intersemiotic cohesion for those attentive viewers who will be able to recognize the Ben & Jerry's ice cream tubs scattered on the floor.

*Implicature*  61

Although no cultural substitutions were observed in the data set originally examined by Desilla (2009), it is hoped that the supplementary analysis of the Italian subtitles for the Ben & Jerry's example, as well as the quick diachronic glance at the handling of that particular utterance into Greek, has brought into sharp relief that the treatment of implicatures crucially depends on the translator's assumptions about the target audience's cognitive environment and, more specifically, the ability of the latter to access certain assumptions at a given moment in time. Whenever ECRs and humour enter the picture, the degree of transculturality/exoticism and intersemiotic cohesion/audiovisual anchoring will need to play a pivotal role (Díaz-Cintas & Remael, 2021).

### 3.4   Exercises and mini research activities

1) Revisit your translations of the Baby Yoda memes from the warm-up exercise:

   - Is there anything that you would change in your first drafts? If so, explain why.
   - Look for any other target versions of these memes on social media or of other Baby Yoda memes and form a mini data set consisting of at least 2 memes in English along with their target versions in your other working languages. How are implicatures handled there? Have a go at analysing them both from a Gricean and an RT perspective.

2) Watch this ad.[7]

   - What are the implicated conclusions of the strapline at the end of the ad? Are they strong or weak? What are the immediate contextual premises triggered by the ad that led you to the implicated conclusions from earlier?
   - How would you translate this strapline in one of your working languages in a hypothetical scenario of localisation/transcreation? Provide two different renderings: one needs to illustrate implicature preservation while the other needs to involve implicature explicitation.
   - The same strapline was used in this older ad.[8] Are the visuals (and the need for intersemiotic cohesion) here more or less restrictive when it comes to the range of translation options available?

3) Watch this short scene fragment[9] from *Bridget Jones: The Edge of Reason* (2004).

   - What instances of implicature can you identify between 00:37–1:32 focusing on Bridget's voice-over? Why do you think the animated jelly fish appears on screen?
   - Have a go at designing a questionnaire (consisting of 3–4 questions) that would test the comprehension of implicit meaning in the jellyfish

# 62  *Navigating interpersonal meaning and communicative styles*

scene by an English-speaking audience. Be prepared to share it with the rest of the class and justify your choice of questions.

- Download and read *Experimental Pragmatics Meets Audiovisual Translation: Tackling Methodological Challenges in Researching How Audiences Understand Implicatures* by Desilla (2019a),[10] which offers guidance on questionnaire design when testing implicature comprehension. Would you make any changes to the first draft of your questionnaire? Why/why not?
- Look for any subtitled or dubbed versions of the film dialogue utterances in question in any of your working languages. How are implicatures rendered there? To what extent does the TT interpretatively resemble the original? What translation strategies can you observe? Alternatively, produce your own target version and reflect on the approach opted for.

## 3.5  Suggestions for further reading

*On language indirectness:*

Lee, J.J., & Pinker, S. (2010) 'Rationale for Indirect Speech: The Theory of the Strategic Speaker', *Psychological Review* 117(3): 785–807.
Terkourafi, M. (2011) 'The Puzzle of Indirect Speech', *Journal of Pragmatics* 43(11): 2861–2865.
Thomas, J. (1995) *Meaning in Interaction. An Introduction to Pragmatics*, London: Longman.

*On the concept of implicature:*

Cummings, L. (2023) *Introducing Pragmatics: A Clinical Approach*, Oxon and New York: Routledge, Chapter 2.
Grice, H.P. (1975) 'Logic and Conversation', in P. Cole & J. Morgan (eds.), *Syntax and Semantics 3: Speech Acts*, New York: Academic Press, 41–58. Reprinted in S. Davis (ed.) (1991) *Pragmatics: A Reader*, Oxford and New York: Oxford University Press, 305–315.
Sperber, D., & Wilson, D. (1995) *Relevance: Communication and Cognition*. 2nd edition, Oxford: Blackwell.
Wilson, D., & Sperber, D. (2004) 'Relevance Theory', in L.R. Horn & G. Ward (eds.), *The Handbook of Pragmatics*, Oxford: Blackwell.

*On implicature in various media:*

Koike, D.A., & César Félix-Brasdefer, J. (2020) *The Routledge Handbook of Spanish Pragmatics*, Abingdon: Routledge, Chapters 1 and 23.
Piskorska, A., & Walaszeska, E. (2017) *Applications of Relevance Theory: From Discourse to Morphemes*, Newcastle upon Tyne: Cambridge Scholars Publishing, Parts III and IV.
Scott, K. (2022) *Pragmatics Online*, Oxon and New York: Routledge, Chapter 6.
Yus, F. (2003) 'Humor and the Search for Relevance', *Journal of Pragmatics* 35(9): 1295–1331.
Yus, F. (2016) *Humour and Relevance*, Amsterdam: John Benjamins.

*Implicature*  63

## On implicature and translation:

Baker, M. (2011) *In Other Words: A Coursebook on Translation*, Oxon and New York: Routledge, Chapter 7.

Desilla, L. (2012) 'Implicatures in Film: Construal and Functions in Bridget Jones Romantic Comedies', *Journal of Pragmatics* 44(1): 30–35. https://doi.org/10.1016/j.pragma.2011.10.002

Desilla, L. (2014) 'Reading Between the Lines, Seeing Beyond the Images: An Empirical Study on the Comprehension of Implicit Film Dialogue Meaning Across Cultures', *The Translator* 20(2): 194–214. https://doi.org/10.1080/13556509.2014.96747

Desilla, L. (2019a) 'Experimental Pragmatics Meets Audiovisual Translation: Tackling Methodological Challenges in Researching How Audiences Understand Implicatures', in R. Tipton & L. Desilla (eds.), *The Routledge Handbook of Translation and Pragmatics*, Oxon and New York: Routledge, 93–114.

Desilla, L. (2019b) 'Happily Lost in Translation: Misunderstandings in Film Dialogue', *Multilingua: Journal of Cross-cultural and Interlanguage Communication* 39(2): 601–618. https://doi.org/10.1515/multi-2018-0123

Galai, F. (2022) *Relevance Theory in Translation and Interpreting: A Cognitive-Pragmatic Approach*, New York: Routledge.

Gutt, E.A. (2000) *Translation and Relevance: Cognition and Context*. 2nd edition, Manchester: St. Jerome Publishing.

## Notes

1  https://ifunny.co/picture/kyzHgByJ8
2  https://www.reddit.com/r/BabyYoda/comments/gad0nr/but_i_want_cookies/?rdt=44953
3  The terms *implicature* and *implicatum* refer roughly to the process and product of implying (i.e., what is implied) respectively (1975/1991: 305–306).
4  The other types of maxim non-observance include *violation*, whereby a speaker unostentatiously fails to observe a maxim in order to deceive or mislead, *opting out*, whereby a speaker chooses neither to observe the maxim nor the CP (e.g, in the utterance "My lips are sealed"), and *clash*, whereby one maxim is violated for the sake of fulfilling another (Grice, 1975/1991: 310).
5  Adapted from Desilla (2019b: 249).
6  It should be borne in mind that the description provided here is based on Sperber and Wilson's (2004) and Carston's (2002a) analysis of analogous examples and, as they admit, is an oversimplified account of the comprehension process (Wilson & Sperber, 2004: 617).
7  https://www.youtube.com/watch?v=4VhUGcEiHT4
8  https://www.youtube.com/watch?v=4fZoIw7qplM
9  https://www.youtube.com/watch?v=9EDAE2IU-eg
10  This chapter can be downloaded from the Sample Chapters Section of the Routledge Translation Studies Portal http://routledgetranslationstudiesportal.com/sample-chapters.php

## References

Asimakoulas, D. (2004) 'Towards a Model of Describing Humour Translation: A Case Study of the Greek Subtitled Versions of *Airplane!* and *Naked Gun*', *Meta* 49(4): 822–842.

Atlas, J.D. (2005) *Logic, Meaning, and Conversation: Semantic Indeterminacy, Implicature, and Their Interface*, Oxford and New York: Oxford University Press.

## 64 Navigating interpersonal meaning and communicative styles

Avramides, A. (1989) *Meaning and Mind*, Cambridge, MA: The MIT Press.

Baby Yoda Biscotti [Digital Image] Retrieved from *Baby Yoda Italia*. Available at: www.facebook.com/babyyodait/ (Accessed date: 4 December 2023).

Baby Yoda Cookies Meme 1 [Digital Image]. (2021) Available at: https://ifunny.co/picture/kyzHgByJ8 (Accessed date: 4 December 2023).

Baby Yoda Cookies Meme 2 [Digital Image]. (n.d.) Available at: www.reddit.com/r/BabyYoda/comments/gad0nr/but_i_want_cookies/?rdt=44953 (Accessed date: 4 December 2023).

Bach, K., & Harnish, R.M. (1987) 'Relevant Questions', *Behavioural and Brain Sciences* 10(4): 711–712.

Baker, M. (2006) 'Contextualisation in Translator- and Interpreter-Mediated Events', *Journal of Pragmatics* 38: 321–337.

Baker, M. (2011) *In Other Words: A Coursebook on Translation*, Oxon and New York: Routledge.

BBC Teach. (n.d.) Love Means . . . Available at https://www.bbc.co.uk/teach/school-radio/articles/zkx7m39 (Accessed date: 12 May 2024).

Blakemore, D. (1987) *Semantic Constraints on Relevance*, Oxford: Blackwell.

Blakemore, D. (1992) *Understanding Utterances*, Oxford: Blackwell.

Brumark, A. (2005) 'Non-Observance of Gricean Maxims in Family Dinner Table Conversation', *Journal of Pragmatics* 38(8): 1206–1238.

Carston, R. (1988) 'Implicature, Explicature and Truth-Conditional Semantics', in M. Kempson (ed.), *Mental Representations*, Cambridge: Cambridge University Press, 155–181.

Carston, R. (1998) 'The Semantics/Pragmatics Distinction: A View from Relevance Theory', *UCL Working Papers in Linguistics* 10.

Carston, R. (2002a) 'Linguistic Meaning, Communicated Meaning and Cognitive Pragmatics', *Mind and Language* 17(1/2): 127–148.

Carston, R. (2002b) *Thoughts and Utterances: The Pragmatics of Explicit Communication*, Oxford: Blackwell.

Carston, R., et al. (2002) 'Introduction: Special Issue on Pragmatics and Cognitive Science', *Mind and Language* 17(1): 1–2.

Chapman, S. (2005) *Paul Grice, Philosopher and Linguist*, Hampshire: Palgrave Macmillan.

Clark, H.H. (1987) 'Relevance to What', *Behavioural and Brain Sciences* 10(4): 714–715.

Cooren, F., & Sanders, R.E. (2002) 'Implicature: A Schematic Approach', *Journal of Pragmatics* 34: 1045–1067.

Cummings, L. (2023) *Introducing Pragmatics: A Clinical Approach*, Oxon and New York: Routledge.

Dascal, M. (1983) *Pragmatics and the Philosophy of Mind I: Thought in Language*, Amsterdam: John Benjamins.

Dascal, M. (2003) *Interpretation and Understanding*, Amsterdam and Philadelphia: John Benjamins.

Davis, W.A. (1998) *Implicature*, Cambridge: Cambridge University Press.

Delabastita, D. (1994) 'Focus on the Pun: Wordplay as a Special Problem in Translation Studies', *Target* 6(2): 223–243.

Delabastita, D. (1996) *Word Play and Translation*, Manchester: St Jerome.

Desilla, L. (2005) *Approaching Audiovisual Translation from a Pragmatic Perspective; Implicature in Subtitling and Dubbing Children's Films for Greek Audiences*. A dissertation submitted to the University of Manchester for the degree of MA.

Desilla, L. (2009) *Towards a Methodology for the Study of Implicatures in Subtitled Films: Multimodal Construal and Reception of Pragmatic Meaning Across Cultures*, Unpublished doctoral thesis, University of Manchester.

Desilla, L. (2012) 'Implicatures in Film: Construal and Functions in Bridget Jones Romantic Comedies', *Journal of Pragmatics* 44(1): 30–35. https://doi.org/10.1016/j.pragma.2011.10.002

Desilla, L. (2014) 'Reading Between the Lines, Seeing Beyond the Images: An Empirical Study on the Comprehension of Implicit Film Dialogue Meaning Across Cultures', *The Translator* 20(2): 194–214. https://doi.org/10.1080/13556509.2014.96747

Desilla, L. (2019a) 'Experimental Pragmatics Meets Audiovisual Translation: Tackling Methodological Challenges in Researching How Audiences Understand Implicatures', in R. Tipton & L. Desilla (eds.), *The Routledge Handbook of Translation and Pragmatics*, Oxon and New York: Routledge, 93–114.

Desilla, L. (2019b) 'Pragmatics', in L. Pérez González (ed.), *The Routledge Handbook of Audiovisual Translation Studies*, Oxon and New York: Routledge, 242–258.

Díaz-Cintas, J., & Remael, A. (2007) *Audiovisual Translation: Subtitling*, Manchester: St. Jerome.

Díaz-Cintas, J., & Remael, A. (2021) *Subtitling: Concepts and Practices*, Oxon and New York: Routledge.

Díaz-Pérez, F.J. (2013) 'The Translation of Wordplay from the Perspective of Relevance Theory: Translating Sexual Puns in Two Shakespearian Tragedies into Galician and Spanish', *Meta* 58(2): 279–302. https://doi.org/10.7202/1024175ar

Díaz-Pérez, F.J. (2014) 'Relevance Theory and Translation: Translating Puns in Spanish Film Titles into English', *Journal of Pragmatics* 70: 108–29.

Durant, A., & Lambrou, M. (2009) *Language and Media: A Resource Book for Students*, Oxon and New York: Routledge.

Fauconnier, G. (1986) 'Roles and Connecting Paths', in C. Travis (ed.), *Meaning and Interpretation*, Oxford and New York: Blackwell, 19–44.

Fauconnier, G. (2004) 'Pragmatics and Cognitive Linguistics', in L.R. Horn & G. Ward (eds.), *The Handbook of Pragmatics*, Oxford: Oxford University Press, 657–674.

Gazdar, G. (1979) *Pragmatics: Implicature, Presupposition and Logical Form*, London: Academic Press.

Gibbs, R.W. (1986) 'On the Psycholinguistics of Sarcasm', *Journal of Experimental Psychology General* 115(1): 3–15.

Gibbs, R.W. (1987) 'Mutual Knowledge and the Psychology of Conversational Inference', *Journal of Pragmatics* 11: 561–588.

Gibbs, R.W., & O'Brien, J. (1991) 'Psychological Aspects of Irony Understanding', *Journal of Pragmatics* 16(6): 523–530.

Goffman, E. (1981) *Forms of Talk*, Oxford: Blackwell.

Green, G.M. (1990) 'The Universality of Gricean Interpretation', in *Proceedings of the Sixteenth Annual Meeting of the Berkeley Linguistics Society*, Berkeley, CA, 411–428.

Grice, H.P. (1957) 'Meaning', *Philosophical Review* 66: 377–388.

Grice, H.P. (1975) 'Logic and Conversation', in P. Cole & J. Morgan (eds.), *Syntax and Semantics 3: Speech Acts*, New York: Academic Press, 41–58. Reprinted in S. Davis (ed.) (1991) *Pragmatics: A Reader*, Oxford and New York: Oxford University Press, 305–315.

Grice, H.P. (1986) 'Reply to Richards', in R. Grandy & R.E. Warner (eds.), *Philosophical Grounds of Rationality*, Oxford: Clarendon Press, 45–106.

Grice, H.P. (1998) 'Retrospective Epilogue (Strand Six)', in A. Kasher (ed.), *Pragmatics: Critical Concepts*, London: Routledge, 177–180.

Gutt, E.A. (1998) 'Pragmatic Aspects of Translation: Some Relevance-Theory Observations', in L. Hickey (ed.), *The Pragmatics of Translation*, Clevedon: Multilingual Matters, 41–53.

Gutt, E.A. (2000) *Translation and Relevance: Cognition and Context*. 2nd edition, Manchester: St. Jerome Publishing.

## 66 Navigating interpersonal meaning and communicative styles

Hill, H. (2006) *The Bible at Cultural Cross-Roads: From Translation to Communication*, Manchester: St. Jerome.

Hoggart, R. (1957) *The Uses of Literacy*, London: Penguin.

Jewitt, C. (2013) 'Multimodal Methods for Researching Digital Technologies', in S. Price, C. Jewitt & B. Brown (eds.), *The SAGE Handbook of Digital Technology Research*, SAGE Publications, 250–265. https://doi.org/10.4135/9781446282229

Kasher, A. (1998) 'Conversational Maxims and Rationality', in A. Kasher (ed.), *Pragmatics: Critical Concepts*, London: Routledge, 181–214.

Keenan, E.O. (1998) 'The Universality of Conversational Postulates', in A. Kasher (ed.), *Pragmatics: Critical Concepts*, London: Routledge, 215–229.

Kidron, B. (Director) (2004a) *Bridget Jones: The Edge of Reason* [Film on DVD including Greek subtitles], Universal Pictures. Released by Videosonic S.A., Greece.

Kidron, B. (Director) (2004b) *Bridget Jones: The Edge of Reason*, Universal Pictures. Retrieved from https://www.netflix.com/gr-en/title/70011203.

Kidron, B. (2004c) *Bridget Jones: The Edge of Reason: The Director's Commentary*. Available at: DVD, UK & USA: Universal Pictures.

Kovačič, I. (1996) 'Subtitling Strategies: A Flexible Hierarchy of Priorities', in C. Heiss & M. Bollettieri Bosinelli (eds.), *Proceedings from the International Conference: Traduzione Multimediale per il Cinema, la Televisione e la Scena*, Forli, 26–28 October 1995.

Kozloff, S. (2000) *Overhearing Film Dialogue*, Berkeley, CA: University of California Press.

Lakoff, G., & Johnson, M. (1981) *Metaphors We Live By*, Chicago: University of Chicago Press.

Lee, J.J., & Pinker, S. (2010) 'Rationale for Indirect Speech: The Theory of the Strategic Speaker', *Psychological Review* 117(3): 785–807.

Levinson, S.C. (1983) *Pragmatics*, Cambridge: Cambridge University Press.

Levinson, S.C. (1989) 'A Review of Relevance', *Journal of Linguistics* 25: 455–472.

Levinson, S.C. (2000) *Presumptive Meanings: The Theory of Generalised Conversational Implicature*, Cambridge, MA: The MIT Press.

Maguire, S. (Director) (2001) *Bridget Jones's Diary* [Film on DVD including Greek subtitles], Universal Pictures. Released by Videosonic S.A., Greece.

Marmaridou, S. (2000) *Pragmatic Meaning and Cognition*, Amsterdam and Atlanta: John Benjamins.

Marwick, A. (2013) 'Memes', *Contexts* 12(4): 13–14.

Mey, J.L. (1993) *Pragmatics: An Introduction*, Oxford: Blackwell.

Mooney, A. (2004) 'Co-Operation, Violations and Making Sense', *Journal of Pragmatics* 36: 899–920.

Newmark, P. (1988) *A Textbook of Translation*, Hemel Hempstead: Prentice Hall.

Pedersen, J. (2011) *Subtitling Norms for Television*, Amsterdam: John Benjamins.

Ramière, N. (2006) 'Reaching a Foreign Audience: Cultural Transfers in Audiovisual Translation', *Journal of Specialised Translation* 6. Available at: www.jostrans.org/issue06/art_ramiere.php (Accessed date: 4 December 2023).

Ranzato, I. (2016) *Translating Culture Specific References on Television: The Case of Dubbing*, London: Routledge.

Reboul, A. (1987) 'The Relevance of *Relevance* for Fiction', *Behavioural and Brain Sciences* 10(4): 729.

Recanati, F. (1987) 'Literalness and Other Pragmatic Principles', *Behavioral and Brain Sciences* 10(4): 729–730.

Recanati, F. (1991) 'The Pragmatics of What Is Said', in S. Davis (ed.), *Pragmatics: A Reader*, Oxford and New York: Oxford University Press, 97–118.

Scott, K. (2022) *Pragmatics Online*, Oxon and New York: Routledge.

*Implicature* 67

Solska, A. (2012) 'Relevance-Theoretic Comprehension Procedure and Processing Multiple Meanings in Paradigmatic Puns', in E. Wałaszewska & A. Piskorska (eds.), *Relevance Theory. More than Understanding*, Newcastle upon Tyne: Cambridge Scholars Publishing, 167–182.

Sperber, D., & Wilson, D. (1986) *Relevance: Communication and Cognition*, Cambridge, MA: Harvard University Press.

Sperber, D., & Wilson, D. (1987a) 'Precis of Relevance', *Behavioural and Brain Sciences* 10(4): 697–710.

Sperber, D., & Wilson, D. (1987b) 'Authors' Response: Presumptions of Relevance', *Behavioural and Brain Sciences* 10(4): 736–753.

Sperber, D., & Wilson, D. (1991) 'Loose talk', in S. Davis (ed.), *Pragmatics: A Reader*, Oxford and New York: Oxford University Press, 540–549.

Sperber, D., & Wilson, D. (1995) *Relevance: Communication and Cognition*. 2nd edition, Oxford: Blackwell.

Sperber, D., & Wilson, D. (1998) 'Mutual Knowledge and Relevance in the Theories of Comprehension', in A. Kasher (ed.), *Pragmatics: Critical Concepts*, London and New York: Routledge, 369–384.

Sperber, D., & Wilson, D. (2002) 'Pragmatics, Modularity and Mind-Reading', *Mind and Language* 17: 3–23.

Stanton, A., & Unkrich, L. (Directors) (2004) *Finding Nemo* (Ψάχνοντας τον Νέμο). [Film; 2-disc collector's edition on DVD including the dubbed and subtitled versions into Greek], Pixar and Walt Disney Enterprises.

Tannen, D. (1989) *Talking Voices: Repetition, Dialogue and Imagery in Conversational Discourse*, Cambridge: Cambridge University Press.

Terkourafi, M. (2011) 'The Puzzle of Indirect Speech', *Journal of Pragmatics* 43(11): 2861–2865.

The Depression Project (n.d.). What People With Depression ACTUALLY Mean By "I'm Fine". Available at https://thedepressionproject.com/blogs/news/what-people-with-depression-actually-mean-by-i-m-fine (Accessed date: 12 May 2024).

Thomas, J. (1995) *Meaning in Interaction. An Introduction to Pragmatics*, London: Longman.

Torresi, I. (2021) *Translating Promotional and Advertising Texts*. 2nd edition, Oxon and New York: Routledge.

Valdés, C. (2019) 'Advertising Translation and Pragmatics', in R. Tipton & L. Desilla (eds.), *The Routledge Handbook of Translation and Pragmatics*, Oxon and New York: Routledge, 171–190.

Verschueren, J. (1999) *Understanding Pragmatics*, London: Arnold.

Vinay, J.P., & Darbelnet, J. (1958/1977) *Stylistique Comparee du Francais et l'Anglais: Methode de Traduction*, Paris: Didier. Translated and edited by J. Sager & M.J. Hamel (1995) as *Comparative Stylistics of French and English: A Methodology for Translation*, Amsterdam and Philadelphia: John Benjamins.

Weizman, E. (1989) 'Requestive Hints', in S. Blum-Kulka & J. House (eds.), *Cross-cultural Pragmatics: Requests and Apologies*, Norwood, NJ: Ablex, 71–95.

Wilson, D. (1994) 'Relevance and Understanding', in G. Brown et al. (eds.), *Language and Understanding*, Oxford: Oxford University Press, 35–58.

Wilson, D., & Sperber, D. (1988) 'Representation and Relevance', in M. Kempson (ed.), *Mental Representations*, Cambridge: Cambridge University Press, 133–153.

Wilson, D., & Sperber, D. (2004) 'Relevance Theory', in L.R. Horn & G. Ward (eds.), *The Handbook of Pragmatics*, Oxford: Blackwell.

Yus, F. (2003) 'Humor and the Search for Relevance', *Journal of Pragmatics* 35(9): 1295–1331.

Yus, F. (2016) *Humour and Relevance*, Amsterdam: John Benjamins.

## 68 *Navigating interpersonal meaning and communicative styles*

Yus, F. (2018) 'Identity-Related Issues in Meme Communication', *Internet Pragmatics* 1(1): 113–133.

Yus, F. (2021) 'Pragmatics and Humor in Spanish Research', in D.A. Koike & J.C. Félix-Brasdefer (eds.), *The Routledge Handbook of Spanish Pragmatics*, Abingdon: Routledge, 403–420.

Yus Ramos, F. (1998) 'A Decade of Relevance Theory', *Journal of Pragmatics* 30: 305–345.

Zappavigna, M. (2012) *Discourse of Twitter and Social Media: How We Use Language to Create Affiliation on the Web*, London: Bloomsbury Academic.

Zenner, E., & Geeraerts, D. (2018) 'One Does Not Simply Process Memes: Image Macros as Multimodal Constructions', in E. Winter-Froemel & V. Thaler (eds.), *Cultures and Traditions of Wordplay and Wordplay Research*, Berlin and Boston: De Gruyter, 167–194. https://doi.org/10.1515/9783110586374-008

### Filmography

*Bridget Jones's Diary* (2001) Sharon McGuire, UK and USA.
*Bridget Jones: The Edge of Reason* (2004) Beeban Kidron, UK and USA.
*Finding Nemo* (2003) Andrew Stanton, Pixar Animation Studios/Walt Disney Pictures.

# 4 (Im)politeness
## A weapon wielded for better or worse

### 4.1 Warm-up

Watch the clip from *Vicky Cristina Barcelona* (Woody Allen, 2008) available at www.youtube.com/watch?v=ih6Baoop5G4. If you are not familiar with the film, please visit www.imdb.com/title/tt0497465/ first for a trailer and plot summary.

- How do the characters come across in this scene fragment? Try to come up with at least two adjectives for each and explain your viewpoint. Would you consider them polite/impolite and on what grounds?
- What is the role of speech acts in character construction and how do they serve the intentions of Vicky, Cristina, and Juan Antonio?

### 4.2 Key concepts

#### 4.2.1 Politeness, face, and threats

Most introductions to politeness tend to start by underscoring the complexity of the phenomenon while forewarning that the kind of politeness that pragmatists are interested in is not really the same as the one that sociolinguists concentrate on. Usually this disclaimer is accompanied by a second (albeit directly related) one: the perception of politeness within pragmatics differs considerably from common perceptions of politeness. It is likely that upon being asked what politeness is, a lay person may touch upon issues pertinent to *deference* (e.g., the choice between tu/vous in French, du/Sie in German, tu/Lei in Italian, and tú/usted in Spanish, as well as address forms and honorifics like Sir/Madam, Professor, etc.); this is indeed the aspect of politeness mainly studied within sociolinguistics and encompasses more of "a moral or psychological disposition towards being nice to one's interlocutor" (Thomas, 1995: 178). Nevertheless, recent studies have revealed that people's responses to what politeness is can be

DOI: 10.4324/9781003213178-6

# 70 *Navigating interpersonal meaning and communicative styles*

much more sophisticated than what a mere "being nice/respectful/considerate to others" would indicate. In her case study of conceptualisations of politeness in Greek which draws on evidence from Twitter, Sifianou (2015: 4) reports that "there is vast disagreement and ample manifestation of diametrically opposing views" including both positive and negative evaluations: for example, politeness is portrayed, *inter alia*, as "the lubricant of social contact", "a very strong weapon", and "a way of exploiting human beings" (cf. Watts, 2003). The view that "expressing feigned politeness is worse than impoliteness" was also found in the sample and will be revisited later in the present chapter. Interestingly enough, the aforementioned portrayals are all in accord with the kinds of politeness explored within pragmatics. *A priori* and out of context politeness is neither positive nor negative; it is a weapon whose powers can be wielded for better or worse, for instance to insult, make amends, negotiate, manipulate, and fall in (and out) of love.

The *first-wave approaches* to politeness research includes the seminal publications of Lakoff (1973), Leech (1983), and Brown and Levinson (1978/1987). In 1996, Culpeper's work propelled a gradual shift of focus from politeness to impoliteness which had been rather neglected until then. Section 4.2.2 will present Brown and Levinson's highly influential approach to politeness while Section 4.2.3 will be dedicated to impoliteness mainly in the light of Culpeper (1996, 2005). Before proceeding to these two sections, it is important to first define the concepts of *face* and *face-threatening acts* which are the building blocks of both theories.

The concept of *face* as proposed by Goffman (1967) is central in Brown and Levinson's politeness theory (1978/1987) and can be defined as "every individual's feeling of self-worth or self-image" (Thomas, 1995: 169). Face can be maintained, enhanced, damaged, and/or repaired through interaction and this applies to both of its aspects: *positive* and *negative*. Our *positive face* reflects our desire to be liked and approved of by others while our *negative face* reflects our desire to have the freedom to act as we choose and not to be imposed upon. The tension between these two different desires across the characters is palpable in the excerpt from *Vicky Cristina Barcelona* (Woody Allen, 2008) on which the warm-up exercise of this chapter is based. The reactions of Vicky and Cristina to Juan Antonio's offer/invitation package to Oviedo speak volumes about which aspect of face is prioritised at any given moment.

As Brown and Levinson (1978/1987) explain, speech acts can potentially threaten another person's positive or negative face. The term for these linguistic threats is *face threatening acts (FTAs)*. Some representative examples of FTAs feature in Table 4.2.1 organised in terms of participant (speaker or addressee) and the particular aspect of face (positive or negative) threatened in each case.

This table can be used as a guide for identifying the FTAs in the excerpt from *Vicky Cristina Barcelona*.

*(Im)politeness* 71

*Table 4.2.1* Examples of FTAs (Adapted from Brown and Levinson, 1987: 65–68)

|  | *Speaker* | *Addressee* |
|---|---|---|
| Threat to Positive Face | • apologies<br>• acceptance of compliments<br>• admissions of guilt/ responsibility | • expressions of criticism/ disapproval/contempt<br>• complaints<br>• disagreements<br>• challenges |
| Threat to Negative Face | • expressing thanks<br>• accepting apologies/offers<br>• excuses<br>• unwilling promises and offers | • requests<br>• orders<br>• threats<br>• warnings<br>• offers/invitations<br>• promises<br>• compliments |

### 4.2.2 Politeness strategies

As shown earlier, face is inevitably vulnerable in the course of everyday inter-action to various kinds of linguistic threats. In Brown and Levinson's frame-work (1978/1987), politeness is perceived as a means to disarm, mitigate, or soften this "aggression"; for them politeness is essentially *redressive action* taken as some sort of a proactive antidote to any undesirable perlocutionary effects of face-threatening acts (FTAs). This conceptualisation underlies their taxonomy of strategies for performing FTAs which comprises three sets of *on-record* superstrategies and one set of *off-record* strategies.

More specifically, if a speaker does choose to proceed with an FTA, the fol-lowing four possibilities emerge: performing the FTA without any redress (*bald on record*), performing the FTA on record with redress using positive polite-ness, performing the FTA with redress on record using negative politeness, and performing the FTA with off-record politeness. Before finalising the choice of a particular strategy, the size or "weightiness" (Thomas, 1995: 169) of the FTA is factored in. The size of the FTA in question is calculated on the basis of three parameters: power, distance, and rating of the imposition (Brown & Levinson, 1978/1987). Of course, if the stakes are too high, a speaker may decide that the best course of action would be to refrain from performing the FTA in whatever shape or form. Brown and Levinson cater for this possibility with *Do Not Per-form the FTA*, which features as the final strategy in their taxonomy.

As Thomas (1995) explains, speakers tend to opt for performing the FTA bald on record, (i.e., speaking directly and/or bluntly) on the following occa-sions: in an emergency or a situation when time is of the essence, when the FTA is perceived as being in the addressee's interest, when the degree of the FTA appears small, when the speaker is more powerful than the addressee, or when the speaker intends to be blatantly offensive. The other three pos-sibilities in performing an FTA, along with their respective substrategies, are presented in Table 4.2.2, where S stands for Speaker and H for Hearer.

72  *Navigating interpersonal meaning and communicative styles*

*Table 4.2.2* Taxonomy of Politeness Strategies (Adapted from Brown and Levinson 1987: 102, 130, 214)

| | *Positive Politeness Strategies* | *Negative Politeness Strategies* | *Off-Record Strategies* |
|---|---|---|---|
| 1 | **Claim common ground**<br>• Notice/attend to H (e.g., interests, wants, needs)<br>• Exaggerate (interest, approval, sympathy with H)<br>• Intensify interest to H<br>• Use in-group identity markers<br>• Seek agreement<br>• Avoid disagreement<br>• Presuppose/raise/assert common ground<br>• Joke | **Be conventionally indirect** | **Violate Relevance**<br>• Give hints<br>• Give association clues<br>• Presuppose |
| 2 | **Convey that S and H are co-operators**<br>• Assert or presuppose S's knowledge of and concern for H's wants<br>• Offer, promise<br>• Be optimistic<br>• Include both S and H in the activity<br>• Give (or ask for) reasons<br>• Assume or assert reciprocity | **Don't presume/assume**<br>• Question, hedge | **Violate Quantity**<br>• Understate<br>• Overstate<br>• Use tautologies |
| 3 | **Fulfil H's want**<br>• Give gifts to H (e.g., goods, sympathy, understanding, cooperation) | **Don't coerce H**<br>• Be pessimistic<br>• Minimise the imposition<br>• Give deference | **Violate Quality**<br>• Use contradictions<br>• Be ironic<br>• Use metaphors<br>• Use rhetorical questions |
| 4 | | **Communicate S's want not to impinge on H**<br>• Apologise<br>• Impersonalise S and H (avoid the pronouns "I" and "you")<br>• State the FTA as a general rule<br>• Nominalise | **Violate Manner**<br>• Be ambiguous<br>• Be vague<br>• Over-generalise<br>• Displace H<br>• Be incomplete, use ellipsis |
| 5 | | **Redress other wants of H's derivative from negative face**<br>• Go on record as incurring a debt or not as indebting H | |

# (Im)politeness 73

Upon closer inspection of the table, it becomes evident that positive politeness strategies are *approach-based*, emphasising closeness and solidarity; they appeal to the addressee's positive face. Negative politeness strategies, by contrast, appeal to the addressee's negative face and are, thus, *avoidance-based*, designed to maintain the distance between interactants (Sifianou, 2001: 131–132). Off-record politeness, on the other hand, arises from *maxim violation/ flouting* (Grice, 1975/1991) and is therefore intimately linked with the generation of implicatures. As a result, off-record politeness carries all the advantages (as well as shortcomings) of conversational indirectness mentioned in Chapter 3.

Let us now consider the following email excerpts which exemplify politeness strategies in action (Alvanoudi & Desilla, 2022).

---

**Example 1**

a) Dear Dr X, . . . I thought you would be interested in this: Z recently opened a YouTube channel full of lectures on G. Maybe you would like to check it out. It seems like a great tool and maybe it will also help us in this semester in our X class!

b) Stay safe from mass propaganda and guard yourself at all times [laughing emoji].

c) The thing is, that the last few months I am experiencing some extreme difficulties with my personal life (apart from the pandemia) and due to the school's obligations as well as my professional ones, I never had nor have the time to rest, give sometime to myself to resolve them and move on. . . . I feel sorry for disappointing you, but I really try my best even under those circumstances. I am sure that sooner or later I will come around.

d) Λόγω της παρούσας κατάστασης του κορωνοϊού δεν είμαι ιδιαίτερα παρών στην πανεπιστημιακή ζωή και καταλαβαίνω πως με έχει καταστρέψει, αλλά δεν μπορώ να αποδίδω όπως θέλω. Προφανώς όλα αυτά είναι δικαιολογίες αλλά και να μην ήταν, πάλι σε μειονεκτική θέση είμαι. [Due to the current COVID situation I have not been very present in university life and I understand that this has destroyed me but I cannot perform as I would have liked to. Obviously, these are all excuses but even if they aren't I am still at a disadvantage.]

---

Alvanoudi and Desilla (2022) explore politeness strategies and manifestations of affect in the context of email discourse between university students and teaching staff. The data obtained cover a significant period of the COVID-19 pandemic (March 2020 until January 2021) and comprise redacted excerpts from emails written either in English or in Greek by undergraduate students addressing their lecturers at the School of English Language and Literature

## 74  Navigating interpersonal meaning and communicative styles

in the Aristotle University of Thessaloniki, Greece. As expected, formality is prevalent across the sample, manifested mainly through the remarkably consistent use of deference markers, including address forms and honorifics (e.g., Dear Dr/Prof) and the formal plural V-form in Greek, as well other negative politeness strategies such as being apologetic and/or thankful (cf. Bella & Sifianou, 2012).

All four excerpts illustrate FTAs since they potentially pose a threat to the lecturer's negative face (Brown & Levinson, 1978/1987). In (1a) the student uses both positive politeness ("it will also help us . . . in our class") and negative politeness mainly in the form of hedging/cautious language ("I thought", "maybe"). However, in (b) the FTA is performed bald on record. The first imperative construction, in particular, ("stay safe from mass propaganda") considerably increases the size of the imposition and, in tandem with the laughing emoji at the end, renders the style of this concluding sentence markedly informal given the power and distance parameters (Alvanoudi & Desilla, 2022). A possible explanation for this finding may pertain to the fact that both public and private discourse have been replete with advice in the interest of the addressee's health along the lines of *take care* and *stay/keep safe* since the outbreak of the pandemic (see Ogiermann & Bella, 2021; Alvanoudi & Desilla, 2022).

Although excerpt (c) is embedded in an email request for coursework extension, no requestive intention whatsoever can be found in the email which includes excerpt (d); the student in the latter apparently felt the need to provide an explanation for his/her poor performance. In (c) negative politeness strategies ("I feel sorry for disappointing you", "the thing is") are combined with positive politeness strategies ("I am sure that sooner or later I will come around") while off-record politeness seems to be the prevalent strategy in (d) ("this has destroyed me", "these are all excuses but even if they aren't I am still at a disadvantage" (Alvanoudi & Desilla, 2022)).

Interestingly enough, both (c) and (d) also illustrate *self-politeness*, a term coined by Chen (2001) whereby "the student risks his[/her] own positive face which [s/]he simultaneously tries to save by mentioning an unavoidable problem" (Bella and Sifianou, 2012: 100). The two senders present themselves as conscientious and committed students admitting that they are struggling with academic performance while providing the COVID-19 pandemic as a cause. *Inter alia*, they touch upon mental health and other personal information which may be considered oversharing in an academic context. Vulnerability (Brown, 2006) more often than not occurs in relationships characterised by intimacy and trust and, thus, this oversharing between a student and a lecturer is a threat to the addressee's negative face since it can cause feeling of uneasiness or even embarrassment (cf. Coates, 2003: 341).

So far we have seen how impoliteness works in monolingual communication. What happens, though, when there is a mediator between speaker

*(Im)politeness* 75

and addressee? Drawing on data, *inter alia*, from educational interpreting, Vargas-Urpi (2019) delves into politeness strategies and face management across cultures.

In a simulated role-play of an interpreted parent-teaching meeting where the original text source-text (ST) is in Catalan and the text produced by the interpreter target-text (TT) is in Chinese, the tutor suggests that the boy should not continue with high school; this act of discouraging is an FTA because it goes against the wishes and preferences of both parent and child in this scenario (Vargas-Urpi, 2019: 349). The original FTA in Catalan is performed largely bald on record ("he does not have it to go to high school"), as opposed to the TT where the Chinese interpreter uses negative politeness ("to go to high school . . . would be a bit difficult") (Vargas-Urpi, 2019: 349–350). What is also striking is the interpreter's addition of a contextualising clause, i.e. "considering the situation of the child now" (ibid: 350). The latter can be considered a positive politeness strategy: by emphasising the "now", the interpreter allows for the possibility that the student could improve in the future, thus demonstrating a degree of (indirect) optimism which can be also traced in the rather comforting added explanation that the student is struggling because he is a new comer (Vargas-Urpi, 2019: 350). The afore-described redressive strategies suggest that the interpreter is particularly concerned with the size of the FTA and takes an active role in face management. It is no surprise that in Chesterman's (1997) model of translation strategies such omissions and additions fall under *pragmatic strategies* and are, thus, instances of *text manipulation*.

Although it could be claimed that such politeness shifts "challenge the notion of accuracy as promoted in PSI [public service interpreting] codes of ethics" (Vargas-Urpi, 2019: 350), they are definitely worth analysing from a cross-cultural pragmatics perspective, not least because there is substantial variation in the way face is perceived, valued, and managed across cultures (Spencer-Oatey, 2002, 2008; cf. Hickey & Stewart, 2005; cf. Bayraktaroglu & Sifianou, 2004; Jackson, 2014: 258–260). Despite Brown and Levinson's aspiration that their model of linguistic politeness can account for cross-cultural differences, their approach has been criticised as susceptible to ethnocentrism (see Matsumoto, 1988; Spenser-Oatey, 2002). Although the idea of categorising cultures into *negative politeness-oriented* and *positive politeness-oriented* may seem appealing at first glance and, indeed helpful to the analyst, such a crude distinction cannot capture the full complexity of the phenomenon and its application often proves problematic (Hickey & Stewart, 2005: 5).

Another criticism articulated against Brown and Levinson (1978/1987) pertains to the underlying premise that politeness strategies are mutually exclusive (Thomas, 1995: 176). The examples examined so far amply demonstrate that negative politeness can perfectly co-exist with positive politeness. But how about a more 'extreme' mix-and-match of strategies?

76  *Navigating interpersonal meaning and communicative styles*

**Example 2**

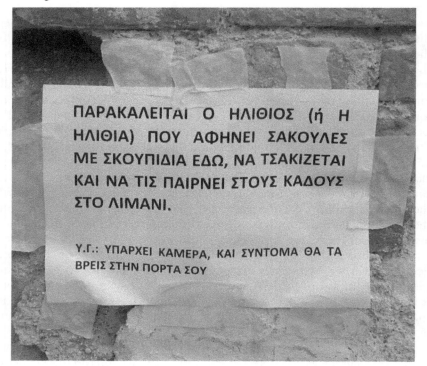

[The idiot [masculine] (or the idiot [feminine]) who leaves garbage bags here is kindly requested to get his/her ass to the port and take them to the garbage bins over there.
P.S.: There is a camera and you will soon find them at your door]

Example 2 is actually a photograph of a paper notice on a street wall on the island of Corfu taken by the author in 2018. The anonymous sender deftly exploits the synergy between the bald on-record strategy and negative politeness. Taking into account the offensive, emotionally charged language ("idiot", "to get his/her ass to the port") and the threat in the post scriptum which is conveyed with zero redressive action, one cannot help but reject the hypothesis that the fairly standard, polite formula for requests "is kindly requested" is *bona fide* on this occasion. In fact, this example would fall under what Culpeper (2005) labels *mock politeness* or *sarcasm* and paves the way for our exploration of impoliteness strategies.

### 4.2.3 Impoliteness

Revisiting the last example of section 4.2.2, one may well wonder if it would have been best described as impoliteness rather than mock politeness. Surely, this would be a valid question bringing into sharp relief the intriguing link between politeness and impoliteness.

Under the umbrella of *hostile interpersonal communication*, *verbal aggression*, or *verbal abuse*, impoliteness has attracted the attention of several fields such as psychology, sociology, and communication studies (Culpeper & Hardaker, 2017: 199). Still, for many years, this phenomenon was completely overshadowed by politeness within pragmatic enquiry. It was not until the mid-1990s that linguists considered impoliteness worthy of study in its own right. Since Culpeper's (1996) influential work, research on impoliteness has gained great momentum and is now developing at a mind-boggling rate.

Impoliteness has frequently been described as the "mirror-reflection phenomenon" of politeness (Dynel, 2017: 456). However, Culpeper and Hardaker (2017: 199) caution against such a label, arguing that impoliteness is so much more than a mere "mirror image" or an "antithesis" of politeness; the phrasing of "apparent antithesis" is proposed instead. In a similar vein, impoliteness cannot be reduced to an unintended result of politeness gone wrong (Beebe, 1995; Culpeper et al., 2003). Although the following definition allows for this possibility, it foregrounds the key role of (perceived) intentionality (Culpeper & Hardaker, 2017: 2017; cf. Culpeper, 2005):

> Impoliteness comes about when: (1) the speaker communicates face-attack intentionally, or (2) the hearer perceives behaviour as intentionally face-attacking, or a combination of (1) and (2).

Bousfield's (2008: 38) definition is less flexible since intentionality appears to be a *sine qua non*; having said that, it should be noted that the overwhelming majority of studies thus far have indeed investigated instances of impoliteness when "conflictive verbal face-threatening acts are purposefully delivered unmitigated . . . and/or with deliberate aggression". In this light, he agrees with Culpeper (2005) that *mock impoliteness* (alternatively referred to as *banter*) cannot be considered "genuine impoliteness" (Bousfield, 2007: 211). For instance, name calling between friends or teasing between partners may be a means of reinforcing intimacy and solidarity and have nothing to do with causing real offence (cf. Culpeper & Hardaker, 2017: 208). Therefore, it is important to bear in mind that no utterance is inherently impolite (or polite, for that matter); apart from being culturally conditioned, politeness and impoliteness are crucially context-dependent (Fraser & Nolan, 1981). Accordingly, the relationship between interactants

## 78  *Navigating interpersonal meaning and communicative styles*

and, importantly, the position and emotions of the addressee should not be neglected by analysts.

Impoliteness can evoke a range of emotions which include, but are certainly not limited to, anger, disgust, contempt, and fear as well as embarrassment, guilt, and shame (Culpeper, 2011). Let us now turn to the actual impoliteness strategies can make addressees feel this way (Culpeper, 1996, 2005):

- **Bald on-record impoliteness:** the FTA is performed in a direct, clear, unambiguous, and concise way in circumstances in which face is not irrelevant or minimized
- **Positive impoliteness:** the use of strategies designed to damage the addressee's positive face wants
- **Negative impoliteness:** the use of strategies designed to damage the addressee's negative face wants
- **Off-record impoliteness:** the FTA is performed by means of an implicature but in such a way that one attributable intention clearly outweighs any others
- **Withhold politeness:** the absence of politeness work where it would be expected; for example, failing to thank somebody for a present may be taken as deliberate impoliteness

To these five impoliteness superstrategies, Culpeper (2005) adds one impoliteness meta-strategy, namely **sarcasm or mock-politeness** whereby the FTA is performed with an insincere use of politeness strategies, as illustrated in Example 3, Section 4.2.2.

The different manifestations of positive and negative impoliteness are listed in Table 4.2.3.

In Section 4.2.2, politeness strategies were illustrated, *inter alia*, in the context of email discourse. In a similar vein, we will exemplify impoliteness strategies drawing on data from computer-mediated-communication (CMC) and, in particular, Twitter. Social media have provided researchers of impoliteness with a rich source of data since they often host *negatively marked online behaviours* (NMOB), such as *flaming* and *trolling* (Hardaker, 2017). The common denominator of flaming and trolling resides in their abusive nature. There is one significant difference though: flaming is *reactive*, an exaggerated response to a stimulus, whereas trolling is *proactive*, a provocation in its own right (Hardaker, 2017: 502–503).

As Hardaker (2017: 502) points out, flaming is "an over-reaction to some sort of provocation, whether that is an expletive-laden rant in reply to an unsolicited email or a sarcastic threat in response to a delayed flight".

*(Im)politeness*  79

*Table 4.2.3* Taxonomy of positive and negative impoliteness strategies (Adapted from Culpeper, 1996, 2005)

| | Positive Impoliteness | Negative Impoliteness |
|---|---|---|
| 1 | Ignore or snub the other<br>• e.g., fail to acknowledge the other's presence | Frighten – instil a belief that action detrimental to the other will occur |
| 2 | Exclude the other from an activity | Condescend, scorn, or ridicule – emphasize your relative power |
| 3 | Disassociate from the other<br>• e.g., deny association or common ground with the other | Be contemptuous |
| 4 | Be disinterested unconcerned unsympathetic | Do not treat the other seriously |
| 5 | Use inappropriate identity markers<br>• e.g., use title and surname when a close relationship pertains, or a nickname when a distant relationship pertains | Belittle the other<br>• e.g., use diminutives |
| 6 | Use obscure and secretive language<br>• e.g., mystify the other with jargon, or use a code known to others in the group, but not the target | Invade the other's space – literally e.g., position yourself closer to the other than the relationship permits or metaphorically, e.g., ask for or speak about information which is too intimate given the relationship |
| 7 | Seek disagreement – select a sensitive topic | Explicitly associate the other with a negative aspect – personalize, use the pronouns 'I' and 'you' |
| 8 | Make the other feel uncomfortable<br>• e.g., do not avoid silence, joke, or use small talk | Put the other's indebtedness on record |
| 9 | Use taboo words – swear or use abusive or profane language | Violate the structure of conversation – interrupt |
| 10 | Call the other names – use derogatory nominations | |

Frustrated at the Robin Hood Airport closure due to heavy snow in Doncaster UK, Paul Chambers has tweeted "You've got a week and a bit to get your shit together otherwise I'm blowing the airport sky high!!" having previously suggested that if the adverse weather conditions continued he would "resort to terrorism" in order to fly to Belfast, Northern Ireland (Hardaker, 2017: 502). Chambers, who was initially found guilty of sending a "menacing electronic communication", said he felt "relieved and vindicated" after a High Court hearing in which his conviction was quashed following a second appeal (www.bbc.com/news/uk-england-19009344). The Crown

# 80 *Navigating interpersonal meaning and communicative styles*

Prosecution Service said it would not appeal against this judgement but stressed that the tweet in question *"had the potential to cause real concern* to members of the public, such as those travelling through the airport during the relevant time" (www.bbc.com/news/uk-england-19009344; emphasis added). What is more, despite Chamber's insistence that this was just a "silly joke", and regardless of whether the threat can be perceived as real or not, his message does contain abusive language targeted at the airport officials/staff ("get your shit together"), thus creating the impression that the airport closure was somehow their fault. On these grounds, Chamber's tweet can be regarded as impolite, evidencing three kinds of impoliteness strategies: bald on-record (the blow up threat *per se*), positive (*use taboo words*), and negative (*frighten, put the other's indebtedness on record*).

Chamber's case attracted worldwide media attention and was reported in many different languages. Let us cast a glance at the way his tweet was translated in *Punto Informatico* (Bottà, n.d.), an Italian online newspaper focusing on current news on informatics and technology.

---

**Example 1**

"Merda! L'Aeroporto Robin Hood è chiuso. Vi do poco più di una settimana per sistemare tutto o faccio saltare l'aeroporto per aria!".
[Crap! The Robin Hood airport is closed. I am giving you a bit more than a week to put everything in order or I will blow the airport up!]

---

In the Italian TT, some of the taboo language is preserved intact ("merda") whereas the vulgarity and idiomaticity of "get your shit together" is lost because the idiom has been rendered by means of a *paraphrase* ("sistemare tutto"). As Baker (2011) observes, translation by paraphrase is perhaps the most common technique for rendering idioms but it is not without shortcomings. Although the bald on-record threat is maintained, the Italian tweet is ever so slightly less impolite particularly as far as the use of positive politeness strategies is concerned. Besides, to echo Sidiropoulou (2021: vii), translation is a perfect "laboratory context where im/politeness phenomena manifest themselves through the meaning-transfer practice". News media translation, which very often entails translation of information by non-professionals, (Zanettin, 2021) provides a particularly fruitful ground for investigating shifts along the politeness-impoliteness continuum.

While cross-disciplinary research on the interplay between pragmatics, social media, and translation is still extremely scarce (Desjardins, 2019), in recent years there has been a growing body of studies on (monolingual) face management on Twitter. The last group of examples concluding our discussion of impoliteness are Brazilian hashtags from the corpus of Oliveira and Carneiro (2020):

*(Im)politeness* 81

---

**Example 2**

a) #Fora [#Out or #No]
b) #FodaSe [#FuckYou]
c) #Caguei [#donotgiveashit]

---

*Flaming*

Added at the end of different tweets on current affairs, these hashtags were targeted at Brazilian politicians and public figures, maximising the attack on their positive face (Oliveira & Carneiro, 2020). As in Chamber's flaming tweet, impoliteness is used here to inflict damage. In this case, however, the sender relies exclusively on positive impoliteness strategies: (a) represents a dismissal *(exclude the other from an activity)* (b) is a *curse/ill wish (use taboo language)*, while (c) illustrates the *be disinterested unconcerned unsympathetic* strategy in Culpeper's (1996) taxonomy.

Hopefully, our exposition of politeness and impoliteness in the previous sections has helped with groping towards an understanding of how these phenomena can shape personalities as well as social relationships (cf. Brown & Levinson, 1978/1987: 232). The following case study will concretise this idea even more by elucidating how (im)politeness can contribute to characterisation in film and how subtitling may tamper with pertinent aspects of meaning, thus potentially affecting character perception across cultures (cf. Mason, 2001; Remael, 2003). At the same time, it will bring together theoretical insights from Chapter 3, thus demonstrating how politeness and implicature can work together in character construction.

## 4.3 Case study

The last two decades have seen a boom in studies of (im)politeness in fiction and, in particular, telecinematic discourse (Jucker & Locher, 2017; Dynel, 2017; Sidiropoulou, 2021). Scholars from the field of audiovisual translation (AVT) have embarked on this endeavour (e.g., Mason, 2001; Remael, 2003; Gartzonika & Şerban, 2009; Guillot, 2010, 2012, 2017; Yuan, 2012). Moreover, an emerging research trend pertains to the "dark alleys of strategic communication" (Sorlin, 2017; cf. Austin, 1990; Sifianou, 2012; Holmes & Stubbe, 2014). Sorlin's (2017) study on the Netflix's series *House of Cards* represents one of most recent attempts to investigate the role of (im)politeness in the construction of manipulative discourse.

The present case study establishes Scene 12 of *Ocean's 11*[1] (2001) as a textbook example of covertly aggressive discourse, in which Frank Catton assumes the role of the sly manipulator with Billy Tim Denham being the ignorant target who goes through both physical and emotional distress.

## 82  *Navigating interpersonal meaning and communicative styles*

In particular, the way in which covert aggression is construed through politeness and impoliteness strategies as well as non-verbal cinematic signifiers (e.g., kinesics, gaze, timbre, etc.) is demonstrated in Section 4.3.1 drawing on insights from psychology, film studies, and pragmatics (Brown & Levinson, 1978/1987; Culpeper, 1996/2011). Importantly, the exchange between the two perfectly illustrates the way language is interlinked with important aspects of characterisation, such as power, race, and gender. Besides, as Guillot (2020: 818) remarks, this scene offers an excellent opportunity for appraising "the methodological complexities of researching AVT as cross-cultural mediation". Furthermore, Section 4.3.2 reports on the findings of a reception study designed to test the comprehension of pragmatic meaning, as well as its impact on characterisation, by a sample of Greek viewers and gauge their preferences regarding the subtitling of this scene.

### 4.3.1  *Observational data analysis*

From a film studies perspective, Strong's (2013: 75) account of the scene[2] perfectly encapsulates the covertly aggressive nature of this conversation while touching upon salient aspects of characterisation, such as power, race, and gender:

> Sent to purchase second-hand vans for the heist, Frank intimidates a redneck car dealer into giving him a low price. Having seemingly failed to reach agreement Frank takes the dealers hand to shake goodbye and observed with a smooth purr: "Man, you've got some lovely hands here. Do you moisturize?" Not releasing the hand, Frank embarks on a comic monologue about moisturisers that, in conjunction with his powerful grip, makes the dealer profoundly uncomfortable and serves to manoeuvre him into a generous discount. . . . The scene uses intersecting dimensions of race, culture and language. The dealer, Billy Tim, is coded by name and Southern accent as a type likely to be rendered ill-at-ease by closeness and conversational intimacy with a black man, especially when coupled with the suggestion of physical force. Recognising this, Frank prolongs and magnifies those factors: moving closer, maintaining the grip, stressing his distinctive timbre, and moving the topic to one calculated to make the dealer even more eager to bring the meeting to an end: Frank's sex life – or, as he puts it with a lubricious smile – his 'social agenda'.

As Simon (2010: 44) observes, "the covert-aggressive's dislike of appearing overtly aggressive is as practical as it is face-saving". At first glance, it seems that Frank is polite throughout this interaction. Following Billy Tim's rather adamant statement that he cannot make a better offer for the vans, Frank does not seem annoyed in the least; instead, he resorts to agreeableness ("Well, I understand"), praise ("they are some great little vans you've got there", humour ("Denham like the jean?"), and flattery ("Man you've got some lovely hands here"). These utterances are intended to make Billy Tim

(Im)politeness 83

drop his defences and make him even more vulnerable to the ensuing escalation of his manipulation. Covertly aggressive characters tend to be excellent manipulators; in the literature, they are even described as disarming con-artists. The following list summarises the key attributes of covertly aggressive personalities which are all recognizable in Frank:

- They always want to have their way or to win.
- They always seek power and control over others.
- They can be deceptively civil, charming, and seductive. They know how to 'look good', what to say and do to get people abandon any intuitive mistrust.
- The know how to capitalize on any weakness and . . . how to catch people unaware and unprepared.

(Simon, 2010: 45)

Put differently, in covert aggression "the perpetrator tries to disguise his/her aggressive intentions, in order to avoid retaliation and/or social condemnation" (Björkqvist et al., 1994). To this end covertly aggressive characters have been found to usually opt for a combination of positive reinforcement, negative reinforcement, and/or punishment: according to McGregor and McGregor (2014: 21), positive reinforcement can involve "employing praise, superficial charm or sympathy, excessive apologies, money/gifts, approval, attention, and public displays of emotional responses . . . such as smiling". Negative reinforcement rewards the individual by removing a negative situation while punishment may take the form of nagging, intimidation, and swearing (McGregor & McGregor, 2014: 21–22).

Conversations with covertly aggressive people often resemble a bombardment (McGregor & McGregor, 2014: 18) and this exchange is an excellent case in point: from the compliment onwards, Frank no longer talks with Billy Tim; he rather talks *at* him. This abrupt change of subject from vans to hand lotions takes Billy Tim aback and leaves him nonplussed. To the ignorant person, Frank may seem knowledgeable, affable, or even well-meaning. What is more, he uses self-pity ("I've tried all sorts of branded lotion", "plus, I'm allergic to camphor") which is yet another weapon in the manipulator's arsenal (McGregor & McGregor, 2014: 21). Only by paying attention to the visuals, however, can one find clear evidence of aggression. Importantly, what starts as a courteous, routine handshake turns into an extremely tight grip which climaxes just before Billy Tim offers to reduce the price to 15,000. The physical pain he was under becomes palpable through cinematography, i.e., the close-up on the handshake *per se*, as well as Billy Tim's facial expression and prosody. In the director's commentary, Soderbergh (2002b), confirms that "Bernie [Mac who plays Frank] was really squeezing his hand, that was not an effect . . . that guy's hand was really red". Apart from the editor's skills, the success of this scene is also attributed to Bernie Mac being "hysterical" and the "phenomenal" way in

## 84 *Navigating interpersonal meaning and communicative styles*

which he rolls his eyes after bombarding Billy Tim with all this nonsense (Soderbergh, 2002b).

In Brown and Levinson's (1978/1987) terms, Billy Tim's initial refusal to drop the price down any further can be described as a face-threatening act (FTA) performed with redress using negative politeness ("I am sorry"). Frank, on the other hand, wishes to get what he wants (negative face) while, at the same time, coming across nice (positive face) in order to draw Billy Tim in. In fact, Frank's utterances illustrate all three super strategies proposed by Brown and Levinson (1978/1987), namely *claim common ground, convey that H and S are cooperators,* and *fulfil H's want for understanding and sympathy.* To be more precise, it can be claimed that Frank exhibits a 'dark' kind of politeness (cf. Austin, 1990) whereby the speaker is "only going through the motions of offering options or showing respect for the addressee's feelings"; in reality, the offer "is a façade, the options nonviable and the respect a sham" (Green, 1989: 147). Indeed, research in psychology suggests that cognitive empathy, which can be, *inter alia,* attested by the presence of the mental verb "I understand", can be strategically employed for "darker" purposes such as manipulation and exploitation (Wai & Tiliopoulos, 2012).

Culpeper and Fernandez-Quintanilla (2017) stress that character construction as well as inter-character dynamics can be constructed through both politeness and impoliteness. So far the emphasis has been on Frank's politeness but, upon closer inspection, it becomes obvious that he does not rely exclusively on positive politeness strategies. Rather, he uses a carefully prepared concoction of both politeness and impoliteness strategies to confuse Billy Tim Denham, thus breaking his resistance. This is in accordance with Sorlin's (2017: 137) finding that "manipulative discourse is parasitic on both politeness and impoliteness strategies to various degrees". More specifically, several impoliteness strategies can be observed in Frank's behaviour, such as making use of *secretive language, making the other feel uncomfortable,* and *invading the other's* space (Culpeper, 1996: 357–358) all of which are touched upon in Strong's (2013) reading of Scene 12. It is noteworthy that these strategies are intended to describe both verbal and nonverbal realisations of impoliteness, which makes Culpeper's taxonomy perfectly applicable to this scene. Arguably, Frank's utterance "we all should wear gloves when going to bed, but I found out that that would be a little interference with my . . . 'social agenda', you know what I mean . . . ", is an excellent example of off-record impoliteness, which, in tandem with his rather salacious smile, intense gaze and subsequent wink, gives rise to implicatures about his sex life. At the same time, this observation is in line with Desilla's (2012) findings pertaining to the multimodal construal of implicatures in films and their narrative functions when it comes to characterisation and, particularly, the creation of intimacy between characters. In this case, though, Frank's claim for intimacy is rather intimidating and apparently unwelcome judging from Billy Tim's reactions.

*(Im)politeness* 85

Apart from the aspects of race and gender touched upon by Strong (2013) in his analysis of the scene from a film studies perspective, the sheer oversharing that Frank indulges in (albeit occasionally tempered by implicatures) may also account for Billy Tim's palpable uneasiness. Vulnerability involves sharing feelings and experiences with people who have earned the right to hear them (Brown, 2006); this is clearly not the case here. In this light, oversharing threatens the addressee's negative face since it may cause feelings of embarrassment, uneasiness, and/or discomfort, as Coates (2003) suggests, while at the same time jeopardising the sender's positive face, since the latter runs the risk of being perceived as manipulative (cf. Held, 1989; Bella & Sifianou, 2012). Presumably, then, in this scene from *Ocean's 11* we are witnessing the dark side of vulnerability.

So far the focus has been on elucidating "the dark alleys" of manipulative discourse focusing primarily on *the horizontal level* of filmic communication (Vanoye, 1985), namely the communication between the characters themselves. The reception study presented in Section 4.3.2 shifts the attention to the *vertical level*, i.e., the communication between the filmmakers and the audience[3], and is in keeping with the one of the emerging trends in (im) politeness research which focuses on character perception (cf. Culpeper & Fernandez-Quintanilla, 2017). One of the most fascinating aspects of exploring film reception arguably resides in the diversity and subjectivity of audience response (Hall, 1980; Wharton & Grant, 2005; Phillips, 2000).

### 4.3.2 Reception study

*Participants and method*

Ten postgraduate students in the School of English Language and Literature at the Aristotle University of Thessaloniki, Greece participated in the study, their ages ranging from 23 to 37 years. Seven of the participants were female while three were male, all native speakers of Greek. The participants were in their second semester of study on the Translation-Translation Studies pathway of the Joint Postgraduate Studies Programme (JPPS) "Conference Interpreting and Translation". Per the entry requirements, all students had excellent knowledge of two foreign languages at C2 level, English being one of them. The overwhelming majority were graduates of foreign languages. Also, it should be noted that at the time of experimental study (spring 2019) the students composing the sample had already been exposed to modules on translation theory, practice, and technology. However, they had not attended modules entirely dedicated to subtitling or pragmatics *per se*, with the exception of a very small number who may have elected such modules as part of their undergraduate degree. Nevertheless, it would be neither fair nor helpful to consider this sample as average viewers precisely due to their field of study (translation) and their motivation when it comes to linguistics and intercultural communication which have inevitably affected their responses in the

## 86 *Navigating interpersonal meaning and communicative styles*

present study. Thus, they will be treated as *viewers-cum-translators* not least for the sake of maximum empirical validity. Last but not least, with respect to previous familiarity with *Oceans 11*, seven out of the ten participants reported that they had seen the film before.

The data elicitation method used in the experiment was that of a questionnaire (cf. Desilla 2019). At the beginning of the session, participants were briefed on the overarching goal of the experiment. They were informed that they would be taking part in a study on how viewers understand certain aspects of films through their perception of the original dialogue, visual information, and subtitles. The specific aim of the experiment, i.e., to test for the understanding of pragmatic meaning (including implicatures) and characterisation, was not disclosed to avoid leading their responses.

The questionnaire, which also included a plot summary, was administered in parts corresponding to the three stages of the experimental procedure. In the first stage students were shown the scene with no subtitles on and were given around 15 min. to answer the following three questions[4]:

a) How would you describe the two characters based on their behaviour in this scene? Which features can help you understand some of their thoughts and feelings?
b) Why do you think Frank changes the subject and refers to Billy Tim's hands and moisturising lotions?
c) What do you think Frank means when he says, "Ideally speaking, we all should wear gloves when going to bed, but I found out that there would be a little interference with my social agenda, if you know what I mean"?

In the second stage, the experimenter showed the scene again with the official DVD subtitles (Soderbergh, 2002a) in Greek (Set 1) and asked them to comment on them as follows:

d) How would you assess the first set of subtitles (Set 1)? Please refer to both strengths and weaknesses.

A sample of official set of Greek subtitles (TT1) can be found next, followed by a back translation (BT1) into English:

ST: I've tried all sorts of branded lotion. I even went fragrance-free for a whole year. Now my sister, she uses uh . . . uh . . . uh . . . uh . . . aloe vera with a little sunscreen in it, yeah, and ideally speaking, we all should wear gloves when going to bed, but I found out that that would be a little interference with my . . . "social agenda", you know what I mean . . . .
TT1: Έχω δοκιμάσει τα πάντα. Μέχρι και άοσμες. Η αδελφή μου βάζει . . . αλόη με λίγη/αντιηλιακή προστασία. Κανονικά πρέπει να φοράμε γάντια στο κρεβάτι . . . αλλά αυτό ήταν κακό/για την κοινωνική μου ζωή.

(Im)politeness    87

**BT1:** I've tried everything. Even odorless ones. My sister puts . . . aloe with a little sun protection. As a rule, we should wear gloves in bed . . . but that was bad for my social life.

**TT2:** Έχω δοκιμάσει όλες τις μάρκες. Ακόμα και ενυδατική χωρίς άρωμα για χρόνο. Η αδερφούλα μου βάζει . . . αλόε βέρα με λίγο αντηλιακό. Ιδανικά, πρέπει να φοράμε και γάντια πριν πάμε για νανάκια. Όμως, ανακάλυψα/ότι με εμποδίζουν να . . . εκφραστώ όταν έχω όρεξη για . . . Με νιώθεις, ε?

**BT2:** I have tried all the brands. Even fragrance-free lotion for a year. My sister[dim] puts . . . aloe vera with a little sunscreen. Ideally, we should also wear gloves before we go beddy-byes[dim]. But, I found out that they don't let me . . . express myself when I'm in the mood for . . . You feel me, eh?

As illustrated, the original dialogue (ST) has been more often than not literally translated into Greek. At the same time, instances of condensation and reformulation can also be observed as well as omissions of whole utterances. Largely due to physical constraints of available space and time inherent to this mode of audiovisual translation (AVT) the original verbal soundtrack is inevitably reduced, either partially through condensation, or totally through omission/deletion of lexical items (Díaz-Cintas & Remael, 2007: 146). This may lead though to loss of pragmatic meaning: Hatim and Mason (1997) were the first AVT scholars who studied politeness in AVT, expressing the concern that this aspect of pragmatic meaning may suffer in the target text due to the spatio-temporal limitations specific to subtitling. For instance, subtitlers sometimes have to resort to the change of (indirect) requests into direct imperatives as well as the omission of hedging and modality indicators for the sake of space economy. As a result, characters could come across more or less (im)polite in the subtitles. Needless to say, filmmakers have expressed their resentment at such distortions (Pérez-González, 2014) and, thus, subtitlers are advised to be careful with text reformulations that can have narrative ramifications (Díaz-Cintas & Remael, 2007: 155).

These physical constraints intrinsic to the mode of subtitling may explain, at least in part, the preservation of the implicature pertaining to Frank's sex life by means of a paraphrase: "Κανονικά πρέπει να φοράμε/γάντια στο κρεβάτι . . . αλλά αυτό ήταν κακό/για την κοινωνική μου ζωή ("As a rule, we should wear gloves in bed . . . but that was bad for my social life"). This finding accords with Desilla's (2009, 2014) case study of implicatures in romantic comedies which showed that the majority of the instances of implicatures composing the data set are preserved in the subtitles, while explicitation (partial or total) is only occasionally opted for.

In the third stage of the experimental procedure participants were shown the scene again, this time with a different set of subtitles (featuring as TT2 from earlier) specifically created by the analyst[5] for the purposes of the experiment. Clearly, this set of subtitles is different from the official DVD subtitles in certain respects: firstly, in line with current subtitling trends, they tend to

## 88 Navigating interpersonal meaning and communicative styles

be longer which allows for the inclusion of some utterances that were not catered for in the original DVD subtitles. In addition, an attempt has been made to do more justice to the orality of the original, *inter alia*, through the prevalence of colloquialisms in Frank's lines which aim at decreasing the distance between speaker and addressee. This is further achieved through the strategic use of the second person singular when addressing Billy Tim from one point onwards (as opposed to TT1, in which the formal plural V form was used throughout) which can be regarded as yet another positive impoliteness device (Culpeper, 2011). Equally crucial is the role of the several diminutives, e.g., "αδερφούλα" (sister [diminutive]), "νανάκια" (beddy-byes [diminutive]) in boosting the superficial charm of Frank. Although diminutives in Greek indeed frequently serve as positive politeness markers indicating solidarity and endearment (Sifianou, 1992, 2001), the diminutive in "Τι απαλά που είναι τα χεράκια σου!" (How soft your hands [diminutive] are!), in tandem with the accompanying the proxemics and kinesics mentioned in Section 4.3.1, is intended to heighten the negative impoliteness of the utterance, its disturbing character, and the resulting invasion of Billy Tim's personal space both literally and metaphorically. A similar approach has been adopted in the handling of Frank's oversharing about his "social agenda": although the core content of the implicature is still kept implicit, the rendering "Ιδανικά, πρέπει να φοράμε/και γάντια πριν πάμε για νανάκια. Όμως, ανακάλυψα/ότι με εμποδίζουν να . . . εκφραστώ όταν έχω όρεξη για . . ./Με νιώθεις, ε?" ("Ideally, we should also wear gloves before we go beddy-byes [diminutive]. But, I found out that they don't let me . . . express myself when I'm in the mood for . . . You feel me, eh?") is apparently more explicit and, therefore, more negatively impolite than ST and TT1 alike.

The last two questions essentially prompted the participants to compare and contrast TT1 to TT2 in an attempt to gauge their preference between the two sets of subtitles:

e) How would you assess of the second set of subtitles (TT2)? Please refer to both strengths and weaknesses.
f) Which set of subtitles would you prefer (TT1 or TT2)? Please justify your answer.

It should be stressed that the two subtitle sets were labelled as TT1 and TT2 without informing participants which set consists of the official DVD subtitles of the film.

*Participant responses*

The first most striking finding to emerge from the data analysis is that the covertly aggressive/manipulative nature of the interaction was sufficiently clear to all participants from the very first stage of the experimental procedure. Needless to say, their answers varied in terms of focus, precision, completeness, and/or explanatory force but overall there was substantial evidence of their ability to recognise most of the key attributes of covertly aggressive personalities in Frank's character leading to Billy Tim's victimisation. The following responses are excellent cases in point:

- PA6: Frank: a manipulator – he knows how to use body language to manipulate his interlocutor so that he gets the desired result. Billy: naïve, lack of confidence, gives in under minor pressure, not in a position to support the power and prestige he exudes – only at first glance.

- PA10: **Frank** **Bill**
  Beginning: friendly but reserved    Beginning: friendly, professional
  Middle: friendly, likable, flatterer    Middle: friendly, disengaged
  End: aggressive, insidious, sly    End: naïve, weak
  Overall: clever, sly    Overall: vulnerable, scared

Interestingly enough, the account of PA10 succinctly captures character development over the course of this scene as well as the key shift in Billy Tim's emotional state.

As expected, a recurrent theme in the data is that of power and control; it is noteworthy that for approximately one third of participants the reversal of power was brought about by a combination of two factors: Frank's hard-to-follow utterances and the painfully tight grip of Billy Tim's hand. Consider these responses:

- PA4: In the beginning, the salesman behaves in a formal and polite manner while Frank appears to listen carefully. When he finishes with his offer, Frank appears to agree and extends his hand for a handshake. On the pretense that he has very soft hands, he tight squeezes his hand for a long time while, at the same time, he tells incoherent stories that make him look scarier (like a psychopath). Eventually, he succeeds in intimidating him and achieve his goal, namely the lower price for the vans.
- PA9: Billy Tim Denham appears to be the classic salesperson with feigned politeness and with a southern accent which creates the image of a polite, and perhaps a bit stupid, person. Frank has the façade of a polite customer who, nevertheless, succeeds in becoming threatening by squeezing the hand while casually talking about hand lotions.

On the whole, the overwhelming majority recognised this superficially haphazard turn in the conversation as a covertly aggressive tactic whose aim is "to mislead Denham" and "cover the fact that he keeps on squeezing his hand". Moreover, two participants felt that Frank's compliment "you've got some lovely hands, here" served as means to "predispose his interlocutor positively" and "to come across friendly and make Billy lower his guard so that he can achieve a better deal".

90  *Navigating interpersonal meaning and communicative styles*

The third question in this first stage of the experiment examines whether the participants can understand the implicatures evoked by Frank's original line in English, "Ideally speaking, we all should wear gloves when going to bed, but I found out that there would be a little interference with my social agenda, if you know what I mean". We should bear in mind that this line manifesting off-record impoliteness is accompanied by Frank's wink and smile as well as the disturbingly prolonged handshake. Notwithstanding these rather powerful immediate contextual premises, this utterance proved rather challenging; less than half of the participants were able to treat the utterance as a sexual innuendo. The attested difficulty in interpreting "social agenda" as intended by the filmmakers (i.e., sex life) was not a complete surprise largely due to the meaning potential of the expression as well as its rather counterintuitive mapping (social/public vs. private/intimate). Indeed, some participants evidently misunderstood Frank's utterance because they accessed unintended context.

Interestingly enough, what all these responses have in common is the link between gloves and criminal activity. Albeit unintended in the present scene, the activation of these implicatures is not completely unwarranted since Frank Catton was a con-artist and the inside man in the casino heist. These observations reflect those of Desilla (2014) who also found that viewers do not always understand implicatures as filmmakers would like them to and that accessing unintended context is a possible scenario which may have a detrimental effect to the comprehension of the utterance as a whole.

With the above in mind, let us now turn to the second and third stages of the experimental procedure which were concerned with subtitle reception. Regarding the official DVD subtitles in Greek (TT1), although the participants overall thought that this was a fairly decent set of subtitles given the physical constraints of space and time, there were some negative comments about the omission of certain utterances while two respondents suggested that the translation was a bit too literal. With respect to the handling of the implicature, participants are anything but unanimous in their views, as illustrated here:

- **PA3:** The threat in the expression "gloves in bed" is distorted.
- **PA5:** Weaknesses: . . . The innuendo of the expression "social agenda" does not become obvious.
- **PA8:** While the innuendo present in the scene was appropriately given; it was preserved as an innuendo and was not given to the audience ready [for consumption].
- **PA9:** Strength: good rendering of "social agenda" as "social life" because it preserves the neutral style with the sexual innuendo.
- **PA10:** I would consider the translation of the expression "a little interference", which has been rendered as "something bad" a minus. Personally, I interpreted the expression in question as "an obstacle", as something negative, but definitely not as "bad".

*(Im)politeness*  91

In contrast to PA8 and PA9 who agree with the subtitler's decision to refrain from spelling out implicit meaning for the audience, PA5 considers this a shortcoming. Although the latter's response is rather cursory, this view may be justified by the (minor) distortions/flattenings highlighted by PA10, namely the rendering of "a little interference" and "social agenda" as "ήταν κακό" (was bad) and "κοινωνική ζωή" (social life), respectively.

Before attempting to interpret these findings, it would be useful to juxtapose them to the participants' views on the treatment of Frank's utterance in the second set of subtitles designed by the analyst:

**PA1:** The misunderstanding of the utterance pertaining to the gloves is a shortcoming.
**PA2:** There are inaccuracies: . . . "social agenda" is conveyed as sexual appetite.
**PA9:** As far as the rendering of "social agenda" is concerned, it preserves "if you know what I mean", however, again, with the innuendo on its own and the triple dots, a part of the dialogue is lost, namely that he says it more formally, giving a knowing look when it comes to the sexual part.
**PA10:** The last part of the interaction, when the offer changes, was accurately and clearly translated.

The responses of PA1 and P2 were reasonably expected given that they both misunderstood Frank's utterance by accessing unintended context, namely associating gloves with criminal activity. The responses of PA9 and P10 are in line with their previous assessment of TT1, obviously for different reasons: PA10 apparently prefers TT2 since it has the accuracy and clarity that TT1 lacks in this case, whereas in PA9's opinion, the lower tenor in TT2 is a weakness.

Overall, it seems that two divergent and often conflicting discourses emerge from the data analysis which is highly indicative of the challenges that implicatures pose to translators. Supposing that the translator has a very strong feeling that the filmmakers mean more or something (entirely) different than what is linguistically encoded in the dialogue, the next step would be to determine this implicit content, which, however, may not be immediately clear. As mentioned in Section 3.2.2, Grice (1975: 315) was one of the first to recognise *indeterminacy* as one of the chief properties of implicatures. As Gutt (2000: 172) notes, the more obscure the interpretation of the original is, the more likely the translator is to misinterpret it. From this angle, spelling out the implicatures in the TT seems to be a risky choice. The subtitles would reflect the translator's own understanding of the implicatures of the original which can be erroneous, since the line between information intended to be implicitly conveyed and wholly unintended information is often a delicate one. Opting for implicature preservation, by contrast, can be viewed as a way of avoiding committing oneself to a particular interpretation, i.e., a way of 'playing it safe', while allowing the audience to make their own inferences at their own peril.

## 92 *Navigating interpersonal meaning and communicative styles*

Apart from the risk it entails, explicitation has several other shortcomings that are intimately linked with the difference between strong and weak communication as well as the open-endedness of implicatures. By means of an implicature meaning is expressed subtly. What is more, according to Relevance Theory, implicatures come in various degrees of strength, enabling the communicator to manipulate the style of the communication at will (Sperber & Wilson, 1995: 199/217). The choice between weak, strong, or no implicature is by no means random, even more so in the context of fictional discourse; it crucially depends on the effect that one intends to achieve as well as the extent to which the active participation of the addressees in the creation of meaning is requested (Desilla, 2012). Given the above, it is conceivable that implicature explicitation in translation is rather undesirable because it upsets the balance between strong and weak communication as realised in the ST and can twist the intended interpretation (Gutt, 2000: 175–176). Care has been taken to avoid this pitfall when creating the second set of subtitles for the purposes of the present study. Admittedly, though, TT2 is less implicit (or more explicit) than TT1 in an attempt to strike a balance between preserving Frank's off-record impoliteness strategy including its communicative advantage of covert aggression and deniability, on the one hand, and increasing the viewers' chances of recovering the intended implicatures while minimising the risk of them being led astray. Still, it is worth underscoring that even such a relatively minor shift on the explicit-implicit continuum might have narrative ramifications in terms of characterisation and/or plot (Desilla, 2012). In Scene 12 of *Ocean's 11* Frank's utterances, in collaboration with non-verbal cinematic signifiers, significantly contribute to the construal of covert aggression, and, thus, linguistic indirectness is a strategic choice on the filmmakers' part. Against this backdrop, opting for a less implicit TT has the potential of rendering the aggression ever so slightly less covert, since the more indirect the utterance, the greater manipulator's leeway for deniability if confronted by the addressee (cf. Sifianou, 2001: 129–130).

Although such an effect was not directly linked by any of the participants to the handling of the implicature in TT2 *per se*, one may discern a relevant hint in the response of one participant who stated, *inter alia*, that the use of the second person singular, colloquialisms, and diminutives "take away the meaning of the scene, which is an apparently very polite dialogue [with] essentially a hidden threat". As anticipated, the tenor shifts which represent positive politeness that were systematically applied during the creation of the second set of Greek subtitles and permeate TT2 elicited mixed responses. Some felt that the translator took too many liberties with the ST while others saw scoring high on the naturalness/idiomaticity scale and catering for the orality of the original in a positive light. This short commentary by PA8 encapsulates the pros and cons of the second set of subtitles, while reflecting the participant's own academic background and affinity with translation studies:

*(Im)politeness* 93

**PA8**: Set 2 had distinctly more idiomatic and stylistic features. Essentially it interpreted the way Frank spoke and attempted to tease out features of his character. This may help convey the humour of this scene and cause more laughter – which, to a degree, is the aim of this scene. On the other hand, such a rendition makes the subtitles much more noticeable and the "translator's invisibility" is lost. The audience is mesmerised by the subtitles and becomes aware of the translator's existence.

The viewers' expectations of faithfulness, in the light of which free renderings would generally seem undesirable, is a recurrent issue in subtitling literature. Target audiences set their own standards for what constitutes successful subtitles and tend to be intolerant to forms of extreme mediation (Bogucki, 2004). Díaz-Cintas and Remael (2021: 76–77) justifiably speak of "the vulnerability of subtitling" compared to other modes of translation: as they explain, as opposed to a translated novel or dubbed programme "subtitles find themselves in the difficult position of being constantly accompanied by film dialogue, giving rise to what in the professional world is known as *the gossiping effect* or *feedback effect* (Törnqvist, 1995)".

Rather unsurprisingly, then, despite overall acknowledging some of the strengths of TT2, six out of the ten participants in the present study stated that they would prefer TT1. Two participants were in favour of TT2, while for the remainder a combination of the two sets of subtitles would be the ideal scenario.

*Case study summary*

Drawing on insights from psychology, film studies, and pragmatics, the case study investigated the construal and reception of covert aggression of Scene 12 of *Ocean's 11* (Soderbergh, 2001) across cultures. As amply demonstrated, the construal of covert aggression in this particular scene is a multimodal enterprise based on the co-deployment of both verbal and non-verbal cinematic signifiers: kinesics, proxemics, haptics, oculesics, vocalics, and cinematography, in tandem with politeness and impoliteness strategies, form the powerful concoction conjured up by the filmmakers to this end. More specifically, positive politeness, negative impoliteness, and off-record impoliteness have been found to significantly contribute to the construal of Frank's covertly aggressive behaviour which leads to Billy Tim's victimisation.

The second set of findings emerges from the experimental case study which aimed at probing the comprehension of pragmatic meaning and characterisation in Scene 12 by a sample of Greek viewers-cum-translators. The most obvious finding to emerge from this study is that all participants understood the covertly aggressive/manipulative nature of their interaction and were overall able to successfully tease out the key features

## 94 *Navigating interpersonal meaning and communicative styles*

of Frank's and Billy Tim's characters, as portrayed in this scene, drawing mainly on film dialogue and the close-up of the painfully firm handshake. As expected, power and control was a dominant theme in their responses. However, Frank's utterance which carries implicatures about his sex life proved difficult for almost half of the participants; evidence suggested that accessing unintended context was more often than not the reason for this misunderstanding. When presented with the option to choose between two sets of Greek subtitles, the majority was rather sceptical towards TT2 which presumably facilitated the recovery of the intended implicatures and used colloquialisms and diminutives to reinforce Frank's superficial charm. Eventually, the preferred TT1 in spite of its extreme text reduction and potentially misleading rendering of Frank's utterance in question. On the whole, there was a sense that the deep-rooted requirement for invisible subtitlers and inconspicuous subtitles is rather at odds with shifts along the implicit-explicit continuum and with boosting the orality and idiomaticity of the TT. Needless to say, it is important to bear in mind the possible bias in these responses given the participants' field of study. There is abundant room for further research in the pragmatics of covert aggression and it is hoped that the present study, despite its exploratory nature and small sample size, offers some insight in this respect.

### 4.4 Exercises and mini research activities

1) Revisit the clip from *Vicky Cristina Barcelona* (Woody Allen, 2008) used in the warm-up exercise of this chapter.

   - Identify the FTAs performed by Juan Antonio, Vicky, or Cristina in this scene.
   - What strategies do the characters use for their FTAs?
   - What could these strategies suggest regarding the way the two cultures (Spanish and American) are portrayed in the film?

2) Have a go at translating Chamber's tweet analysed in Section 4.2.3 in your native/second language. Then, look for any translations already published online. Compare and contrast the different versions focusing on any impoliteness shifts. What translation strategies have resulted in those shifts?

3) Conduct a mini research on manifestations of (im)politeness in the context of Google reviews. A good starting point would be to look for instances in which there is an interaction between the reviewer and a restaurant owner, for instance, who has responded to the review. Discuss the (im)politeness strategies that can be observed in such online exchanges.

4) Read Sorlin's (2017) case study of (im)politeness and manipulation in the Netflix series *House of Cards*. Subsequently, try to find subtitled or

*(Im)politeness* 95

dubbed versions of some of the excerpts analysed by Sorlin in your native/
second language.

- Does Frank Underwoood come across less, more, or equally manipulative in the target language (TL)?
- Can you observe any (im)politeness shifts?

- If so, to what extent can these shifts be attributed to mode-specific constraints (e.g., spatio-temporal constraints in subtitling, lip-sync in dubbing, etc.)?


## 4.5 Suggestions for further reading

*On the concept of politeness:*

Brown, P., & Levinson, S. (1978/1987) *Politeness: Some Universals in Language Usage*, Cambridge: Cambridge University Press.
Fraser, B. (1990) 'Perspectives on Politeness', *Journal of Pragmatics* 14(2): 219–236.
Lakoff, R.T. (1973) *The Logic of Politeness; Or Minding Your P's and Q's*, Chicago: Chicago Linguistics Society.
Leech, G.N. (1983) *Principles of Pragmatics*, London: Longman.
Thomas, J. (1995) *Meaning in Interaction. An Introduction to Pragmatics*, London: Longman, Chapter 6: Theories of Politeness.

*On the concept of impoliteness:*

Bousfield, D. (2008) *Impoliteness in Interaction* (Pragmatics & Beyond New Series 167), Amsterdam: John Benjamins.
Culpeper, J. (1996) 'Towards an Anatomy of Impoliteness', *Journal of Pragmatics* 25: 349–367.
Culpeper, J. (2011) *Impoliteness: Using Language to Cause Offence*, Cambridge: Cambridge University Press.
Spencer-Oatey, H. (2008) 'Face, Impoliteness and Rapport', in H. Spencer-Oatey (ed.), *Culturally Speaking: Culture, Communication and Politeness Theory*. 2nd edition, London: Continuum, 11–47.

*On (Im)politeness in fiction:*

Dynel, M. (2017) '(Im)politeness and Telecinematic Discourse', in M.A. Locher & A. Jucker (eds.), *Pragmatics of Fiction*, Berlin and Boston: De Gruyter Mouton, 455–487. https://doi.org/10.1515/9783110431094
Kizelbach, U. (2017) '(Im)politeness in Fiction', in M.A. Locher & A. Jucker (eds.), *Pragmatics of Fiction*, Berlin and Boston: De Gruyter Mouton, 425–454. https://doi.org/10.1515/9783110431094
Sorlin, S. (2017) 'The Pragmatics of Manipulation: Exploiting Im/politeness Theories', *Journal of Pragmatics* 121: 132–146. https://doi.org/10.1016/j.pragma.2017.10.002

*On (Im)politeness in non-fiction*

Culpeper, J., & Holmes, O. (2013) '(Im)politeness and Exploitative TV in Britain and North America: *The X Factor* and *American Idol*', in N. Lorenzo-Dus & P.G.C. Blitvich (eds.), *Real Talk: Reality Television and Discourse Analysis in Action*, London: Palgrave Macmillan. https://doi.org/10.1057/9781137313461_

## 96 *Navigating interpersonal meaning and communicative styles*

Hardaker, C. (2017) 'Flaming and Trolling', in C.R. Hoffmann & B. Wolfram (eds.), *Pragmatics of Social Media*, Berlin and Boston: De Gruyter Mouton. https://doi.org/10.1515/9783110431070

Oliveira, A.L.A.M., & Carneiro, M.M. (2020) 'A Pragmatic View of Hashtags: The Case of Impoliteness and Offensive Verbal Behavior in the Brazilian Twitter', *Acta Scientiarum. Language and Culture* 42(1), Universidade Estadual de Maringá, Brasil.

### On (Im)politeness and translation

Gartzonika, O., & Şerban, A. (2009) 'Greek Soldiers on the Screen: Politeness, Fluency and Audience Design in Subtitling', in J. Díaz Cintas (ed.), *New Trends in Audiovisual Translation*, Clevedon: Multilingual Matters, 239–250.

Guillot, M. (2010) 'Film Subtitles from a Cross-cultural Pragmatics Perspective: Issues of Linguistic and Cultural Representation', *The Translator* 16(1): 67–92.

Guillot, M. (2017) 'Subtitling and Dubbing Telecinematic Text', in M.A. Locher & A. Jucker (eds.), *Pragmatics of Fiction*, Berlin and Boston: De Gruyter Mouton, 397–424. https://doi.org/10.1515/9783110431094

Hatim, B., & Mason, I. (1997) 'Politeness in Screen Translating', in B. Hatim & I. Mason (eds.), *The Translator as Communicator*, London: Routledge, 65–80.

Hickey, L., & Stewart, M. (eds.) (2005) *Politeness in Europe*, Clevedon: Multilingual Matters.

Mason, I. (2001) 'Coherence in Subtitling: The Negotiation of Face', in F. Chaume Varela & R. Agost (eds.), *La Traducción en los Medios Audiovisuales*, Castelló de la Plana: Servei de Publicacions de la Universitat Jaume I, 19–32.

Remael, A. (2003) 'Mainstream Film Dialogue and Subtitling', *The Translator* 9(2): 225–247.

Sidiropoulou, M. (2021) *Understanding Im/politeness Through Translation: The English-Greek Paradigm*, Cham: Springer.

Valdeón, R. (2017) 'Pragmatics and the Translation of Fiction', in M.A. Locher & A. Jucker (eds.), *Pragmatics of Fiction*, Berlin and Boston: De Gruyter Mouton, 367–396. https://doi.org/10.1515/9783110431094

Vargas-Urpi, M. (2019) 'Public Service Interpreting in Educational Settings: Issues of Politeness and Educational Settings', in R. Tipton & L. Desilla (eds.), *The Routledge Handbook of Translation and Pragmatics*, Oxon and New York: Routledge, 336–365.

Yuan, X. (2012) *Politeness and Audience Response in Chinese-English Subtitling*, Oxford: Peter Lang.

## Notes

1 This scene from *Ocean's 11* and its subtitling/dubbing into French, Italian, German, and Castilian is analysed from other theoretical and methodological perspectives in the special issue of Perspectives (Volume 28, Issue 6, 2020) on *Audiovisual Translation and Interdisciplinarity* (see Guillot, 2020). This work, as part of the Tapping the Power of Foreign Language Films: Audiovisual Translation as Cross-cultural Mediation networking project (2016–2017), was supported by the Arts and Humanities Research Council, (Grant Number: AHRC AH/N007026/1). As co-investigator of this project, I would like to extend my heartfelt thanks to the PI Prof. Marie-Noelle Guillot and all the colleagues involved. I would like to dedicate the case-study analysed in Section 4.3 of this book to them, as I was not able to contribute to the afore-mentioned special issue due to personal circumstances.

# (Im)politeness 97

2 A full transcript of the scene in English is available to download under Supplemental Material on www.tandfonline.com/doi/full/10.1080/0907676X.2020.1753925
3 Messerli (2020) provides an insightful discussion of the communication with viewers in this scene from the perspectives of Grice's cooperative principle and Constitutive Communication Theory.
4 The questionnaire as well as the participants' responses were originally provided in Greek. All the questions and participant responses quoted in Section 4.3.2 are my translations into English, while back-translations into English are provided for Greek subtitles.
5 I would like to thank Mr. Thanos Chrysanthopoulos for his valuable input and assistance.

## References

Alvanoudi, A., & Desilla, L. (2022) 'Exploring the Collateral Impact of the COVID-19 Pandemic on Communication: Displaying Affect in Email Discourse', *Aegean Working Papers in Ethnographic Linguistics* 3: 230–246. Available at: https://ejournals.epublishing.ekt.gr/index.php/awpel/article/view/30237

Austin, P. (1990) 'Politeness Revisited – The Dark Side', in A. Bell & J. Holmes (eds.), *New Zealand Ways of Speaking English*, Philadelphia: Multilingual Matters, 277–293.

Baker, M. (2011) *In Other Words: A Coursebook on Translation*. 2nd edition, London and New York: Routledge.

Bayraktaroglu, A., & Sifianou, M. (eds.) (2004) *Linguistic Politeness Across Cultures: The Case of Greek and Turkish*, Amsterdam: John Benjamins.

Beebe, L.M. (1995) 'Polite Fictions: Instrumental Rudeness as Pragmatic Competence', in J.E. Alatis et al. (eds.), *Linguistics and the Education of Language Teachers: Ethnolinguistic, Psycholinguistic and Sociolinguistic Aspects*, Washington, DC: Georgetown University Press, 154–168.

Bella, S., & Sifianou, M. (2012) 'Greek Student E-mail Requests to Faculty Members', in R.L. de Zarobe & Y. de Zarobe (eds.), *Speech Acts and Politeness Across Languages and Cultures*, Bern: Peter Lang, 89–113.

Björkqvist, K., Österman, K., & Lagerspetz, K.M.J. (1994) 'Sex Differences in Covert Aggression Among Adults', *Aggressive Behavior* 20(1): 27–33. https://doi.org/10.1002/1098-2337(1994)20:1<27::AID-AB2480200105>3.0.CO;2-Q

Bogucki, L. (2004) 'The Constraint of Relevance in Subtitling', *Journal of Specialised Translation* 1: 71–88. Available at: www.jostrans.org/issue01/issue01toc.htm (Accessed date: 4 December 2024).

Bottà, G. (n.d.) 'Se il cinguettio non spaventa nessuno', *Punto Informatico*. Available at: www.punto-informatico.it/se-il-cinguettio-non-spaventa-nessuno/ (Accessed date: 4 December 2023).

Bousfield, D. (2007) '"Never a Truer Word Said in Jest": A Pragmastylistic Analysis of Impoliteness as Banter in Henry IV, Part 1', in M. Lambrou & P. Stockwell (eds.), *Contemporary Stylistics*, London: Continuum, 209–220.

Bousfield, D. (2008) *Impoliteness in Interaction* (Pragmatics & Beyond New Series 167), Amsterdam: John Benjamins.

Brown, B. (2006) 'Shame Resilience Theory: A Grounded Theory Study on Women and Shame', *Families in Society: The Journal of Contemporary Social Services* 87(1): 43–52.

Brown, P., & Levinson, S. (1978/1987) *Politeness: Some Universals in Language Usage*, Cambridge: Cambridge University Press.

Chen, R. (2001) 'Self-politeness: A proposal', *Journal of Pragmatics* 33: 87–106.

Chesterman, A. (1997) *Memes of Translation*, Amsterdam and Philadelphia: John Benjamins.

## 98 Navigating interpersonal meaning and communicative styles

Coates, J. (2003) 'The Role of Epistemic Modality in Women's Talk', in R. Facchinetti, M. Krug & F. Palmer (eds.), *Modality in Contemporary English*, Berlin: Mouton de Gruyter Publishing, 341–348.

Culpeper, J. (1996) 'Towards an Anatomy of Impoliteness', *Journal of Pragmatics* 25: 349–367.

Culpeper, J. (2005) 'Impoliteness and Entertainment in the Television Quiz Show: The Weakest Link', *Journal of Politeness Research: Language, Behaviour, Culture* 1(1): 35–72.

Culpeper, J. (2011) *Impoliteness: Using Language to Cause Offence*, Cambridge: Cambridge University Press.

Culpeper, J., Bousfield, D., & Wichmann, A. (2003) 'Impoliteness Revisited: With Special Reference to Dynamic and Prosodic Aspects', *Journal of Pragmatics* 35(10–11): 1545–1579.

Culpeper, J., & Fernandez-Quintanilla, C. (2017) 'Fictional Characterisation', in M.A. Locher & A. Jucker (eds.), *Pragmatics of Fiction*, Berlin and Boston: De Gruyter Mouton, 93–128. https://doi.org/10.1515/9783110431094

Culpeper, J., & Hardaker, C. (2017) 'Impoliteness', in J. Culpeper, M. Haugh & D. Kadar (eds.), *Palgrave Handbook of (Im)politeness*, Basingstoke: Palgrave, 199–225.

Culpeper, J., & Holmes, O. (2013) '(Im)politeness and Exploitative TV in Britain and North America: *The X Factor* and *American Idol*', in N. Lorenzo-Dus & P.G.C. Blitvich (eds.), *Real Talk: Reality Television and Discourse Analysis in Action*, London: Palgrave Macmillan. https://doi.org/10.1057/9781137313461

Desilla, L. (2009) *Towards a Methodology for the Study of Implicatures in Subtitled Films: Multimodal Construal and Reception of Pragmatic Meaning Across Cultures*, Unpublished doctoral thesis, University of Manchester.

Desilla, L. (2012) 'Implicatures in Film: Construal and Functions in Bridget Jones Romantic Comedies', *Journal of Pragmatics* 44(1): 30–35. https://doi.org/10.1016/j.pragma.2011.10.002

Desilla, L. (2014) 'Reading Between the Lines, Seeing Beyond the Images: An Empirical Study on the Comprehension of Implicit Film Dialogue Meaning Across Cultures', *The Translator* 20(2): 194–214. http://doi.org/10.1080/13556509.2014.967476

Desilla, L. (2019) 'Experimental Pragmatics Meets Audiovisual Translation: Tackling Methodological Challenges in Researching How Audiences Understand Implicatures', in R. Tipton & L. Desilla (eds.), *The Routledge Handbook of Translation and Pragmatics*, Oxon and New York: Routledge, 93–114.

Desjardins, R. (2019) 'Translation, Pragmatics and Social Media', in R. Tipton & L. Desilla (eds.), *The Routledge Handbook of Translation and Pragmatics*, Oxon and New York: Routledge, 375–393.

Díaz-Cintas, J., & Remael, A. (2007) *Audiovisual Translation: Subtitling*, Manchester: St. Jerome.

Díaz-Cintas, J., & Remael, A. (2021) *Subtitling: Concepts and Practices*, London and New York: Routledge

Dynel, M. (2017) '(Im)politeness and Telecinematic Discourse', in M.A. Locher & A. Jucker (eds.), *Pragmatics of Fiction*, Berlin and Boston: De Gruyter Mouton, 455–487. https://doi.org/10.1515/9783110431094

Fraser, B. (1990) 'Perspectives on Politeness', *Journal of Pragmatics* 14(2): 219–236.

Fraser, B., & Nolan, W. (1981) 'The Association of Deference with Linguistic Form', *International Journal of the Sociology of Language* 27: 93–109.

Gartzonika, O., & Şerban, A. (2009) 'Greek Soldiers on the Screen: Politeness, Fluency and Audience Design in Subtitling', in J. Díaz Cintas (ed.), *New Trends in Audiovisual Translation*, Clevedon: Multilingual Matters, 239–250.

Goffman, E. (1967) *Interaction Ritual: Essays on Face-to-Face Behaviour*, Garden City: New York.

*(Im)politeness* 99

Green, G.M. (1989) *Pragmatics and Natural Language Understanding*, Hillsdale, NJ: Lawrence Erlbaum Associates.

Grice, H.P. (1975) 'Logic and Conversation', in P. Cole & J. Morgan (eds.), *Syntax and Semantics 3: Speech Acts*, New York: Academic Press, 41–58. Reprinted in S. Davis (ed.) (1991) *Pragmatics: A Reader*, Oxford and New York: Oxford University Press, 305–315.

Guillot, M. (2010) 'Film Subtitles from a Cross-cultural Pragmatics Perspective: Issues of Linguistic and Cultural Representation', *The Translator* 16(1): 67–92.

Guillot, M. (2012) 'Stylization and Representation in Subtitles: Can Less be More?', *Perspectives* 20: 479–494.

Guillot, M. (2017) 'Subtitling and Dubbing Telecinematic Text', in M.A. Locher & A. Jucker (eds.), *Pragmatics of Fiction*, Berlin and Boston: De Gruyter Mouton, 397–424. https://doi.org/10.1515/9783110431094

Guillot, M. (2020) 'Ocean's Eleven Scene 12: The Sample as Methodological Cogitation – Rationale and Data', *Perspectives* 28(6): 816–821.

Gutt, E.A. (2000) *Translation and Relevance: Cognition and Context*. 2nd edition, Manchester: St. Jerome Publishing.

Hall, S. (1980) 'Encoding/Decoding', in S. Hall et al. (eds.), *Culture, Media, Language*, New York: Routledge, 128–138.

Hardaker, C. (2017) 'Flaming and Trolling', in C.R. Hoffmann & B. Wolfram (eds.), *Pragmatics of Social Media*, Berlin and Boston: De Gruyter Mouton. https://doi.org/10.1515/9783110431070

Hatim, B., & Mason, I. (1997) 'Politeness in Screen Translating', in B. Hatim & I. Mason (eds.), *The Translator as Communicator*, London: Routledge, 65–80.

Held, G. (1989) 'On the Role of Maximization in Verbal Politeness', *Multilingua* 8(2–3): 167–206.

Hickey, L., & Stewart, M. (eds.) (2005) *Politeness in Europe*, Clevedon: Multilingual Matters.

Holmes, J., & Stubbe, M. (2014) *Power and Politeness in the Workplace*, New York: Routledge.

Jackson, J. (2014) *Introducing Language and Intercultural Communication*, London and New York: Routledge.

Jucker, A., & Locher, M.A. (2017) 'Introducing Pragmatics of Fiction: Approaches, Trends and Develoments', in M.A. Locher & A. Jucker (eds.), *Pragmatics of Fiction*, Berlin and Boston: De Gruyter Mouton, 1–21. https://doi.org/10.1515/9783110431094

Kizelbach, U. (2017) '(Im)politeness in Fiction', in M.A. Locher & A. Jucker (eds.), *Pragmatics of Fiction*, Berlin and Boston: De Gruyter Mouton, 425–454. https://doi.org/10.1515/9783110431094

Lakoff, R.T. (1973) *The Logic of Politeness; Or Minding Your P's and Q's*, Chicago: Chicago Linguistics Society.

Leech, G.N. (1983) *Principles of Pragmatics*, London: Longman

Mason, I. (2001) 'Coherence in Subtitling: The Negotiation of Face', in F. Chaume Varela & R. Agost (eds.), *La traducción en los medios audiovisuales*, Castelló de la Plana: Servei de Publicacions de la Universitat Jaume I, 19–32.

Matsumoto, Y. (1988) 'Reexamination of the Universality of Face: Politeness Phenomena in Japanese', *Journal of Pragmatics* 12: 403–426. http://dx.doi.org/10.1016/0378-2166(88)90003-3

McGregor, J., & McGregor, T. (2014) *The Sociopath at the Breakfast Table: Recognising and Dealing with Antisocial and Manipulative People*, Alameda: Hunter House Publishers.

Messerli, T. C. (2020). 'Subtitled artefacts as communication – the case of Ocean's Eleven Scene 12'. *Perspectives* 28(6): 851–863. https://doi.org/10.1080/0907676X.2019.1704805

100  *Navigating interpersonal meaning and communicative styles*

Ogiermann, E., & Bella, S. (2021) 'On the Dual Role of Expressive Speech Acts: Relational Work on Signs Announcing Closures during the Covid-19 Pandemic', *Journal of Pragmatics* 184: 1–17.

Oliveira, A.L.A.M., & Carneiro, M.M. (2020) 'A Pragmatic View of Hashtags: The Case of Impoliteness and Offensive Verbal Behavior in the Brazilian Twitter', *Acta Scientiarum. Language and Culture* 42(1), Brasil: Universidade Estadual de Maringá.

Pérez-González, L. (2014) *Audiovisual Translation: Theories, Methods and Issues*, London and New York: Routledge.

Phillips, P. (2000) *Understanding Film Text: Meaning and Experience*, London: British Film Institute.

Remael, A. (2003) 'Mainstream Film Dialogue and Subtitling', *The Translator* 9(2): 225–247.

Sidiropoulou, M. (2021) *Understanding Im/politeness through Translation: The English-Greek Paradigm*, Cham: Springer.

Sifianou, M. (1992) 'The Use of Diminutives in Expressing Politeness: Modern Greek versus English', *Journal of Pragmatics* 17: 155–173. http://doi.org/10.1016/0378-2166(92)90038-D

Sifianou, M. (2001) *Discourse Analysis: An Introduction*, Athens: Leader Books.

Sifianou, M. (2012) 'Disagreements, Face and Politeness', *Journal of Pragmatics* 44: 1554–1564.

Sifianou, M. (2015) 'Conceptualising Politeness in Greek: Evidence from Twitter Corpora', *Journal of Pragmatics* 86: 25–30.

Simon, G. (2010) *Understanding and Dealing with Manipulative People*, Marion: Purkhurst Brothers Publishers.

Soderbergh, S. (Director) (2002a) *Ocean's 11* [Film on DVD including Greek subtitles], Village Roadshow Pictures, Audiovisual Enterprises, Greece.

Soderbergh, S. (2002b) *Ocean's 11: The Director's Commentary*. Available at: DVD. Greece: Audio Visual Enterprises.

Sorlin, S. (2017) 'The Pragmatics of Manipulation: Exploiting Im/politeness Theories', *Journal of Pragmatics* 121: 132–146. https://doi.org/10.1016/j.pragma.2017.10.002

Spencer-Oatey, H. (2002) 'Managing Rapport in Talk: Using Rapport Sensitive Incidents to Explore the Motivational Concerns Underlying the Management of Relations', *Journal of Pragmatics* 35(5): 529–545.

Spencer-Oatey, H. (2008) 'Face, Impoliteness and Rapport', in H. Spencer-Oatey (ed.), *Culturally Speaking: Culture, Communication and Politeness Theory*. 2nd edition, London: Continuum, 11–47.

Sperber, D., & Wilson, D. (1995) *Relevance: Communication and Cognition*. 2nd edition, Oxford: Blackwell.

Strong, J. (2013) 'Talking Teams: Dialogue and the Team Film Formula', in J. Jaeckle (ed.), *Film Dialogue*, New York: Columbia University Press, 70–84.

Tapping the Power (n.d.) *Tapping the Power of Foreign Language Films: Audiovisual Translation as Cross-cultural Mediation.*

Thomas, J. (1995) *Meaning in Interaction. An Introduction to Pragmatics*, London: Longman.

Törnqvist, E. (1995) 'Fixed Pictures, Changing Words: Subtitling and Dubbing the Film Babette Gæstebud', *TijdSchrift voor Skandinavistik* 16(1): 47–64.

Valdeón, R. (2017) 'Pragmatics and the Translation of Fiction', in M.A. Locher & A. Jucker (eds.), *Pragmatics of Fiction*, Berlin and Boston: De Gruyter Mouton, 367–396. https://doi.org/10.1515/9783110431094

Vanoye, F. (1985) 'Conversations Publiques', *Iris* 3(1): 99–188.

Vargas-Urpi, M. (2019) 'Public Service Interpreting in Educational Settings: Issues of Politeness and Educational Settings', in R. Tipton & L. Desilla (eds.), *The Routledge Handbook of Translation and Pragmatics*, Oxon and New York: Routledge, 336–365.

Wai, M., & Tiliopoulos, N. (2012) 'The Affective and Cognitive Empathic Nature of the Dark Triad of Personality', *Personality and Individual Differences* 52: 794–799. http://doi.org/10.1016/j.paid.2012.01.008

Watts, R. (2003) *Politeness*, Cambridge: Cambridge University Press.

Wharton, D., & Grant, J. (2005) *Teaching Analysis of Film Language*, London: British Film Institute.

Yuan, X. (2012) *Politeness and Audience Response in Chinese-English Subtitling*, Oxford: Peter Lang.

Zanettin, F. (2021) *News Media Translation*, Cambridge: Cambridge University Press. https://doi.org/10.1017/9781108568364

## Filmography

*Ocean's 11* (2001) Steven Soderbergh, Village Roadshow Pictures.

*Vicky Cristina Barcelona* (2008) Woody Allen, Warner Bros Pictures.

# Index

Note: Page numbers in *italics* indicate a figure and page numbers in **bold** indicate a table on the corresponding page.

accuracy 75, 91
advertisement (ad) 16, 23–24, 32
aggression 71; covert 82–83, 92–94; verbal 77
ambiguity 35, 54
anaphora 7, 10–11
antecedent 7
audio-description (AD) 9–13
audio-introductions (AI) 10–12
audiovisual translation (AVT) 9, 11, 21, 81, 82, 87
Austin, J.L. 16, 18–19

back-translation (BT) 86, 97n4
borrowing 53
Brown and Levinson 70–73, 75, 84

cataphora 7
characterisation 7, 81–82, 84, 86, 92–93
cinematic signifiers 82, 92–93
cinematography 12, 56, 83, 93
clickbait 8, 13
cognitive effects 42–44, 46, 47, 50, 52, 53, 55, 56
cognitive empathy 84
cognitive environment 45, 47, 52, 55–56, 61
coherence 39
cohesion 7, 11, 13; intersemiotic 13, 60–61
collocation 53
compensation 59
computer-mediated communication (CMC) 32, 78

condensation 13, 87; *see also* text reduction
conventional implicature 35–36, 42
cooperative principle (CP) 35, 38, 97n3
Culpeper, J. 70, 76–78, **79**, 81, 84
cultural substitutions 60–61

deference 6, 69, **72**, 74
deictic expression 5, 7, 9, 13, 17
deixis 3–14
disambiguation 4, 47–48, 50, 52
discourse deixis 5

editing 12, 56
emotionally charged language 76
enrichment 48–49, 50, 52
entailment 33, 44
explicature 47–50, **50**, 52–54, 57–59
explicitation 57–61, 87, 92
extralinguistic cultural references (ECRs) 58–59, 61

face 70, 75; management 75, 80; negative 70, **71**–72, 73–74, 78, 84–85; positive 70, **71**, 73–74, 78, 81, 84–85; saving strategy 32, 82
face-threatening act (FTA) 70–71, **72**, 77, 84
fictional discourse 55, 92
figures of speech 32, 37, 51
film 4, 7, 10–12, 25, 56–58, 69, 81, 86, 88; audience 6; character 6; dialogue 37, 56, 57, 62, 93, 94; reception 85; studies 82, 85, 93; subtitling 6, 21

*Index* 103

flaming 78, 81
floutings 35–38, 41, 51, 73
force 16–18, 32

gender 10, 82, 85
gossiping effect 93
Grice 32–42, 44–45, 47, 49, 54, 91

hashtags 80–81
humour 5, 41, 46, 52, 59, 61, 82, 93

ideal language philosophy 17–18
idiomaticity 80, 92, 94
illocution 18, 21–22; *see also* force
implicature 31–42; implicated
    conclusions 48–49, 51, 56, 58–61;
    implicated premises 48–51, 53, 56–
    59; strong 49, **50**, 54–56, 58, 61, 92;
    weak 49, **50**, 51–56, 58–59, 61, 92
impoliteness 70, 74, 76–78, **79**, 80–82,
    84, 88, 90, 92–95
indeterminacy 39, 41, 91
indirect speech act 19, 21–22
inference 40–41, 44, 47, 54, 55
innuendo 90–91
intercultural communication 7, 85
interpreting 6, 9, 75, 85, 90; public
    service 75
interpretive resemblance 51–53
intersemiotic translation 9
intimacy 6, 11, 32, 51, 74, 77, 82, 84
irony 32, 37, 41, 46, 51, 58

kinesics 16, 23, 57, 82, 88, 93

linguistic indirectness 31, 59, 92
literal translation 16, 23–24, 57, 87
localisation 23–24, 53, 61; videogame 22
locution 18–19, 32, 48

manipulation 83–84, 94; text 75
maxim 35–41, 51, 55; violation 73
media accessibility 9
mediation 82, 93
meme 6, 31, 46, 52–53
metaphor 32, 37–38, 41, 51–53, 57,
    59, **72**
mise-en-scène 10, 23, 56, 58
mock politeness 76–78
modulation 22
music 12, 16

narration 9–10
negative politeness 71, **72**, 73–76, 84

oculesics 23, 93
omission 21, 75, 87, 90
orality 88, 92, 94
ordinary language philosophy 17–18
origo 6
ostensive inferential communication
    44–46

paraphrase 80, 87
particularised conversational implicature
    (PCI) 36–39, 41
perlocution 18
person deixis 5–8, 11–12
place deixis 5, 7
politeness 32, 40, 69–71, 73
positive politeness 71, **72**, 73–75, 80,
    84, 88, 92–93
processing effort 43–44, 46, 49, 54–55,
    59–60
proposition 4, 47–48
proxemics 23, 88, 93
pun 53, 60

reception 7, 12, 90, 93; study 10, 12,
    82, 85
redressive action 71, 76
reference 5, 7–8, 12–13; assignment 4,
    17, 48, **50**; resolution 47–48, 52
referent 5–6, 11, **50**
relevance 42–43, 47–49, **50**, 52,
    54–56, 60, **72**; cognitive principle
    44–45; communicative principle
    46–47; presumption of optimal
    46–47, **50**
relevance-theoretic comprehension
    procedure 47, 49, **50**, 53, 56
relevance theory 40, 42, 92

sarcasm 41, 59, 76, 78
Searle, J.R. 19, 21, 25
self-politeness 74
social media 3, 18, 52, 61, 78, 80
song 4, 23, 58
speech act 17–19, 21–25
style 10–11, 22, 32, 51, 53, 58, 60, 74,
    90, 92
subtitling 9, 21, 57, 60, 81–82, 85, 87,
    93, 95

104 *Index*

text reduction 60, 94
time deixis 5, 7, 10
transcreation 24, 61
translation 6, 7, 14, 16, 21–25, 32, 52–53, 59–60, 80, 90, 92–94; strategies 62, 75, 94; studies 52, 58, 85, 92

transliteration 60
trolling 78

verbatim translation 19, 57
vulnerability 74, 85; subtitling 93

wordplay 32, 46, 52, 59–60